Magical World of Fantasy Doodles
Coloring & Activity Book

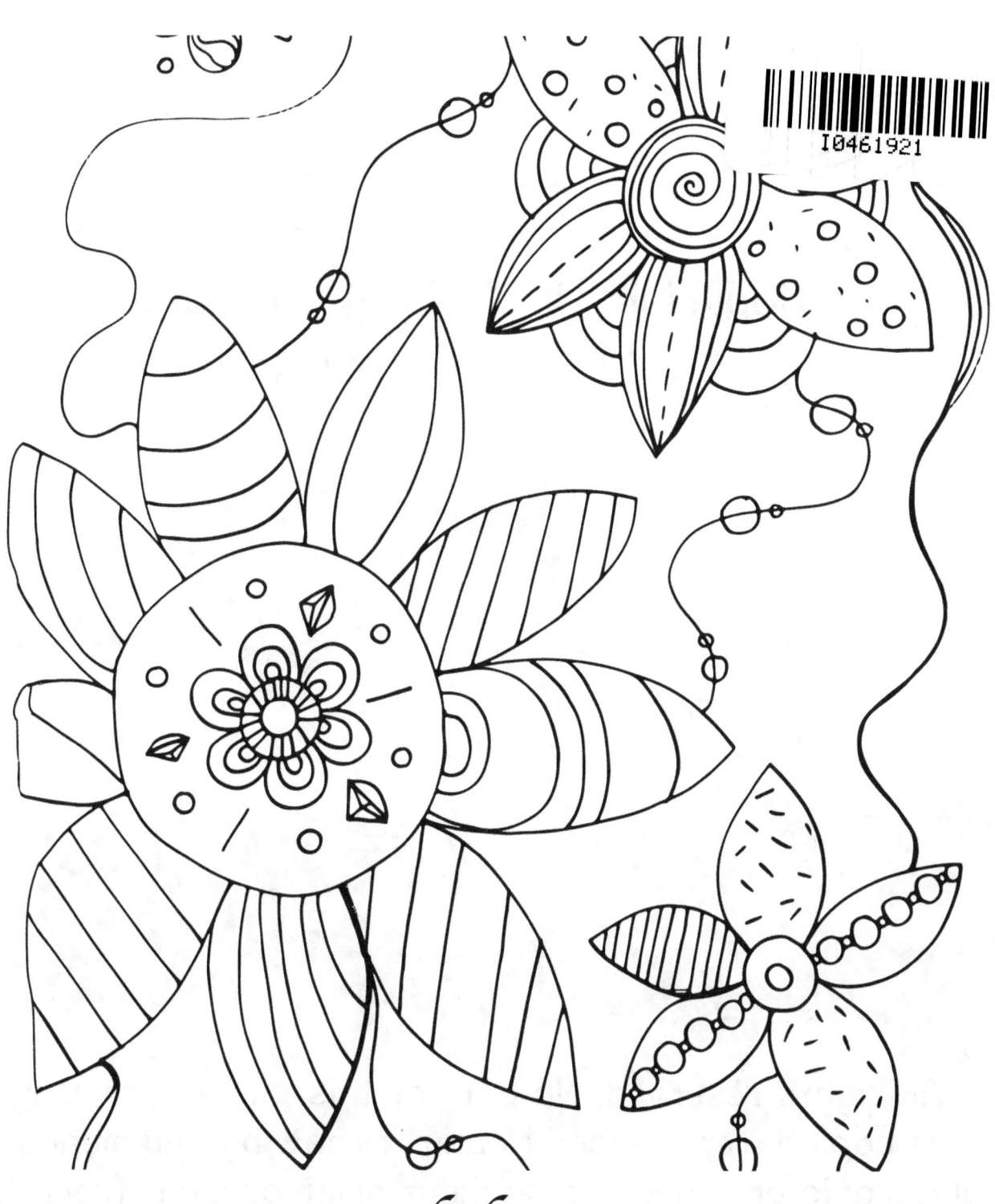

Colokara

Hey!

Let's Start The Relaxing!

Are You Ready To Travel Magical World?

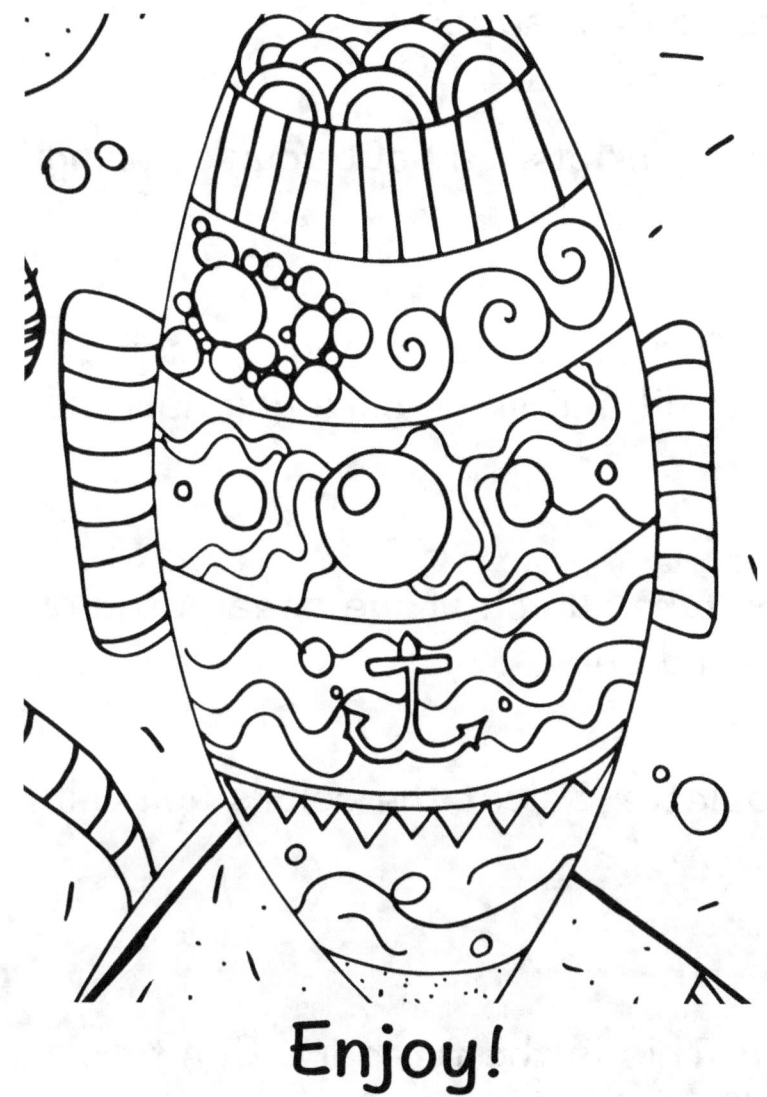

Enjoy!

This book includes a **Free Digital Copy** (PDF format) at the end of this paperback version. It's an awesome gift for you that you could print your favorite images and color them an unlimited number of times.

Steps to a Relaxing Coloring

As an adult, you can enjoy coloring just as much as you did as a child. To make it a truly relaxing experience, try following these steps:

1. Find a quiet space. It's easier to focus on what you are doing when there are no distraction.

2. Organize your materials. Lay out your coloring book and crayons or pens.

3. Set the mood. Turn on some tranquil music, diffuse lavender or another relaxing oil and make sure you have your preferred drink at hand.

4. Select your picture. Which image speaks to you today? That's the one you should color.

5. Choose your palette. Select the colors you will be using for your
    image.

6. Begin coloring. This is the fun part. Don't worry about getting everything perfect, just start.

Allow yourself to relax and focus on the coloring. You'll find it is an amazing way to alleviate stress and take a little time out from the day's hassles. If you feel don't want to do it anymore, just stop!

Color Charts Test

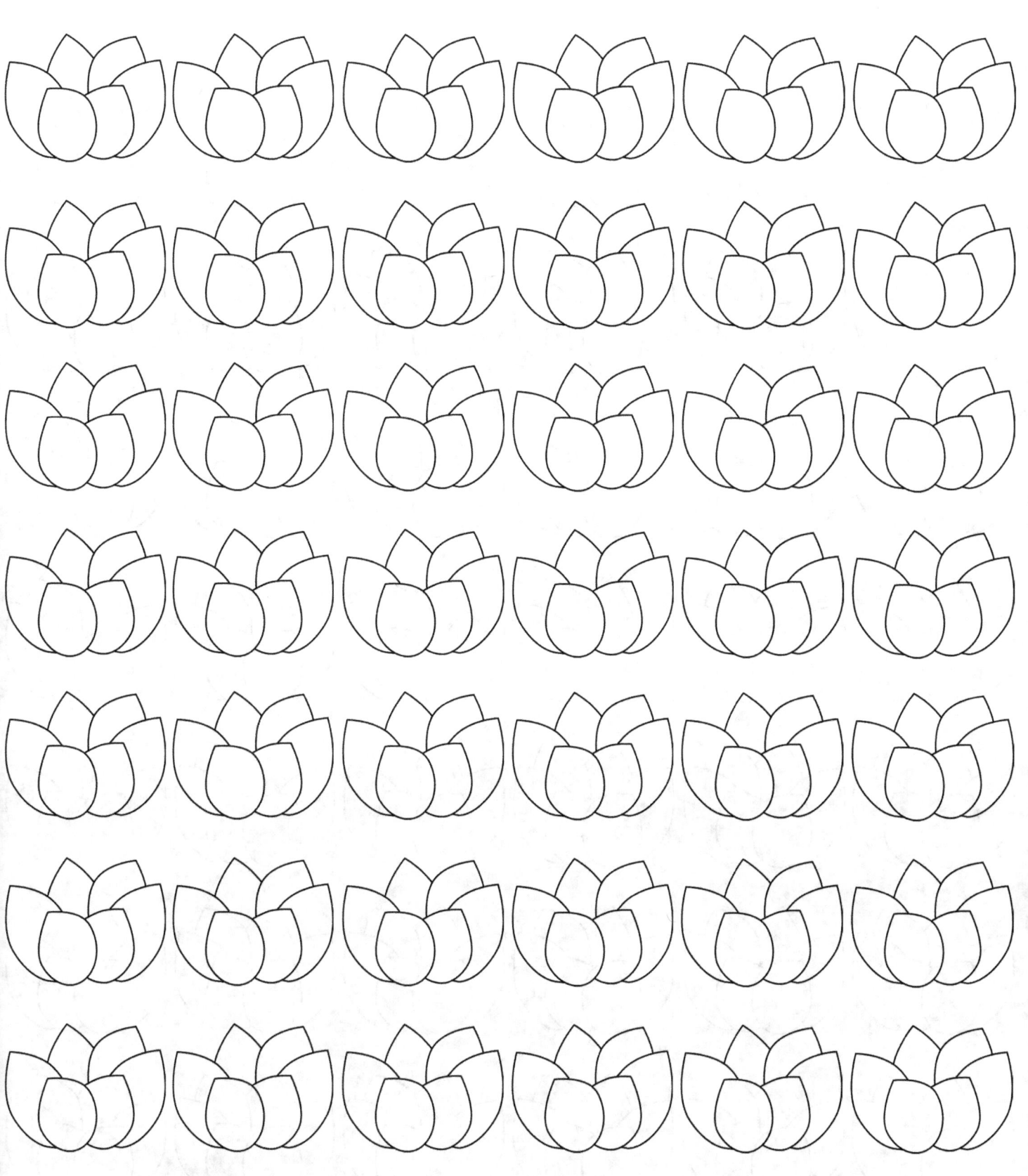

Color Charts Test

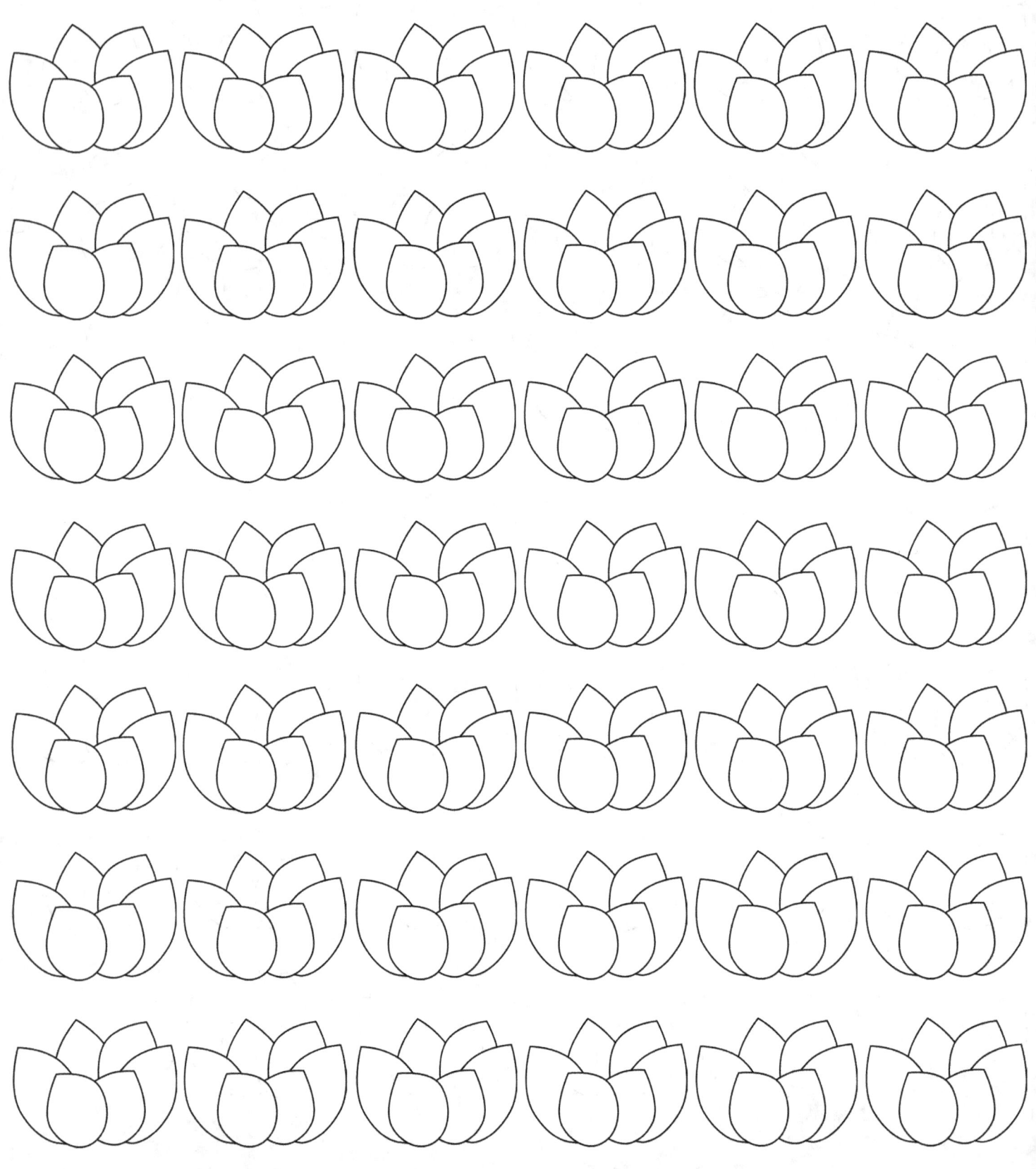

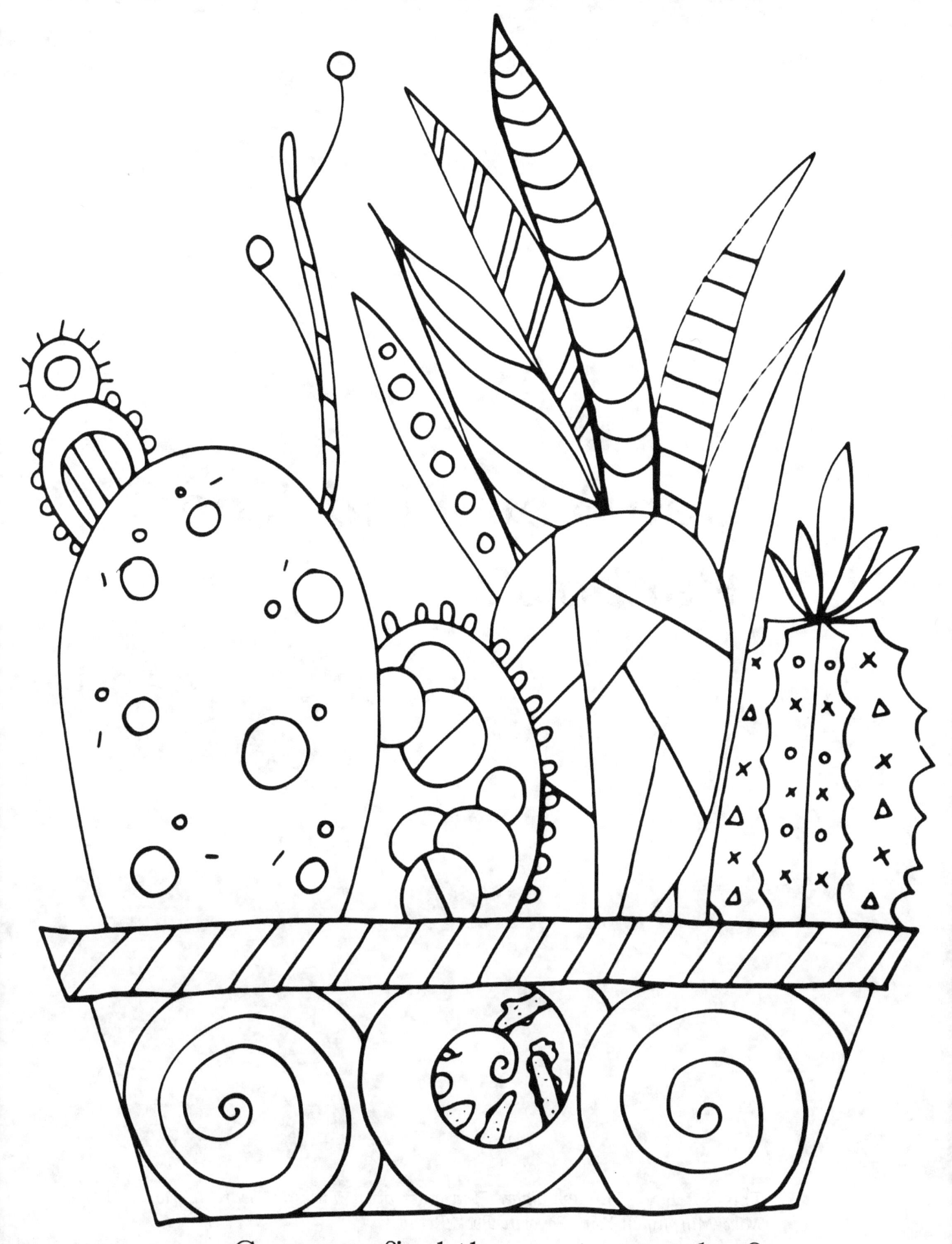

Can you find the cactus cycle ?

Can You Find The Ranbow?

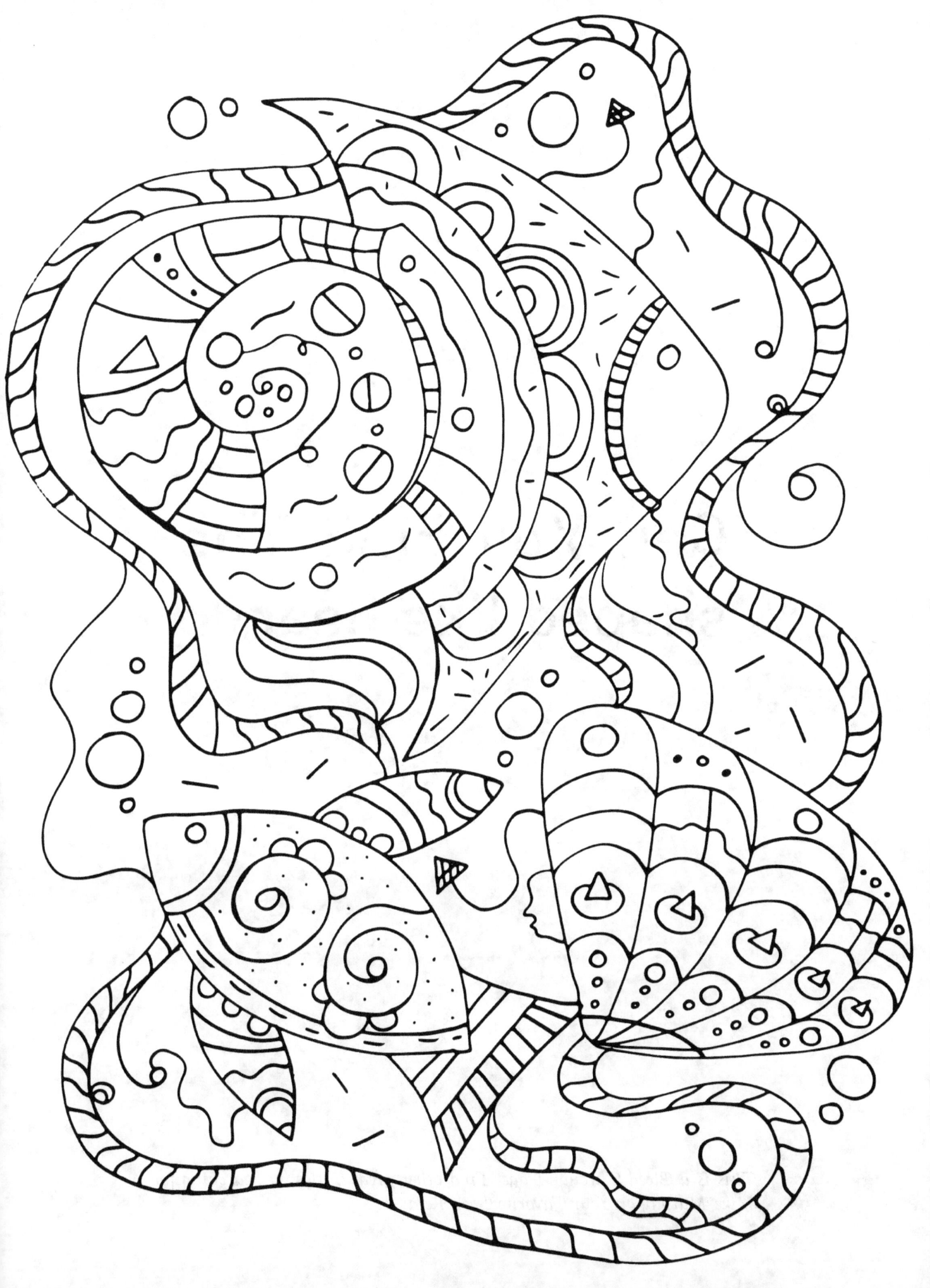

Can You Find The shaped like heart?

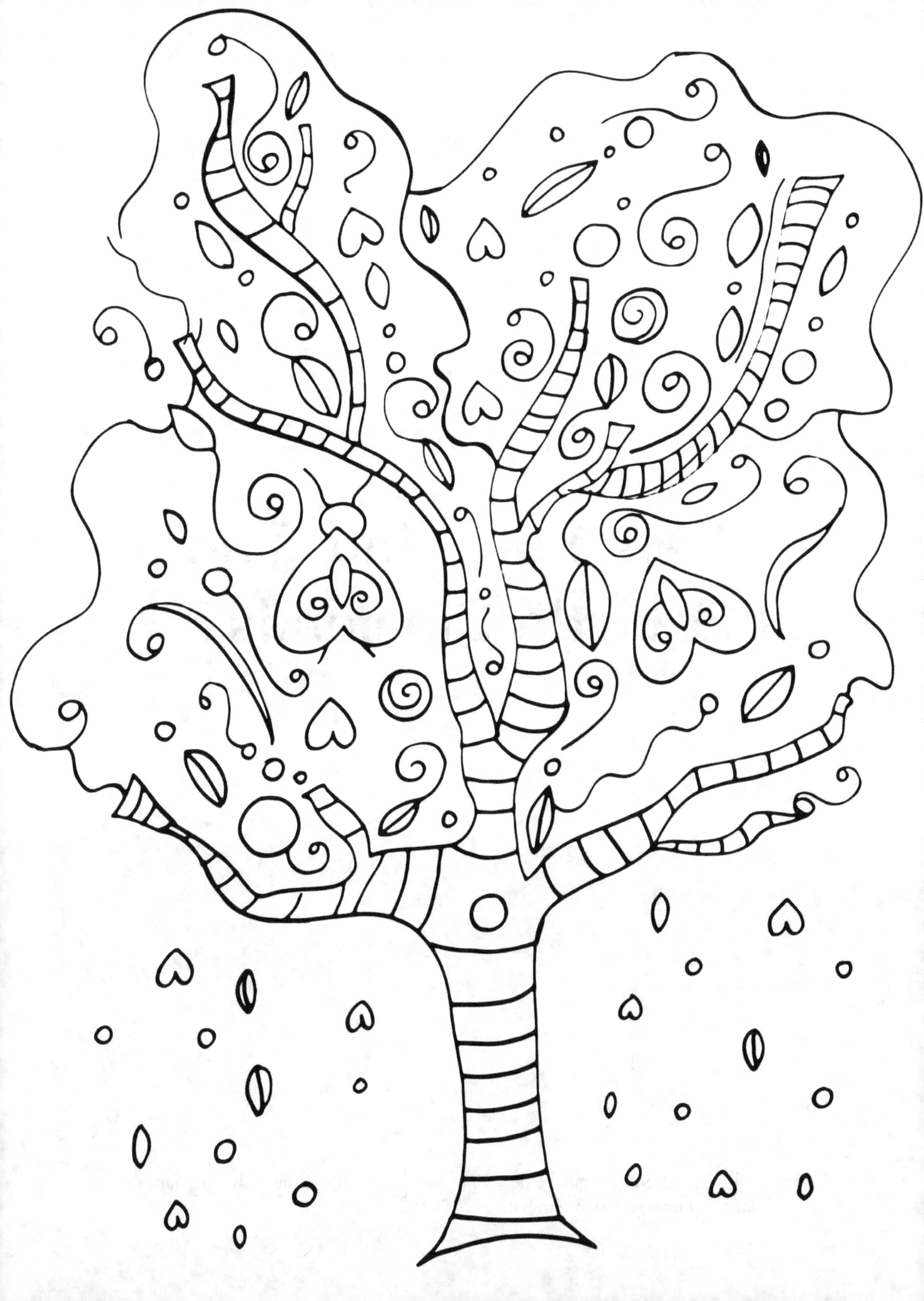

Can You Find The 3 Little Diamonds?

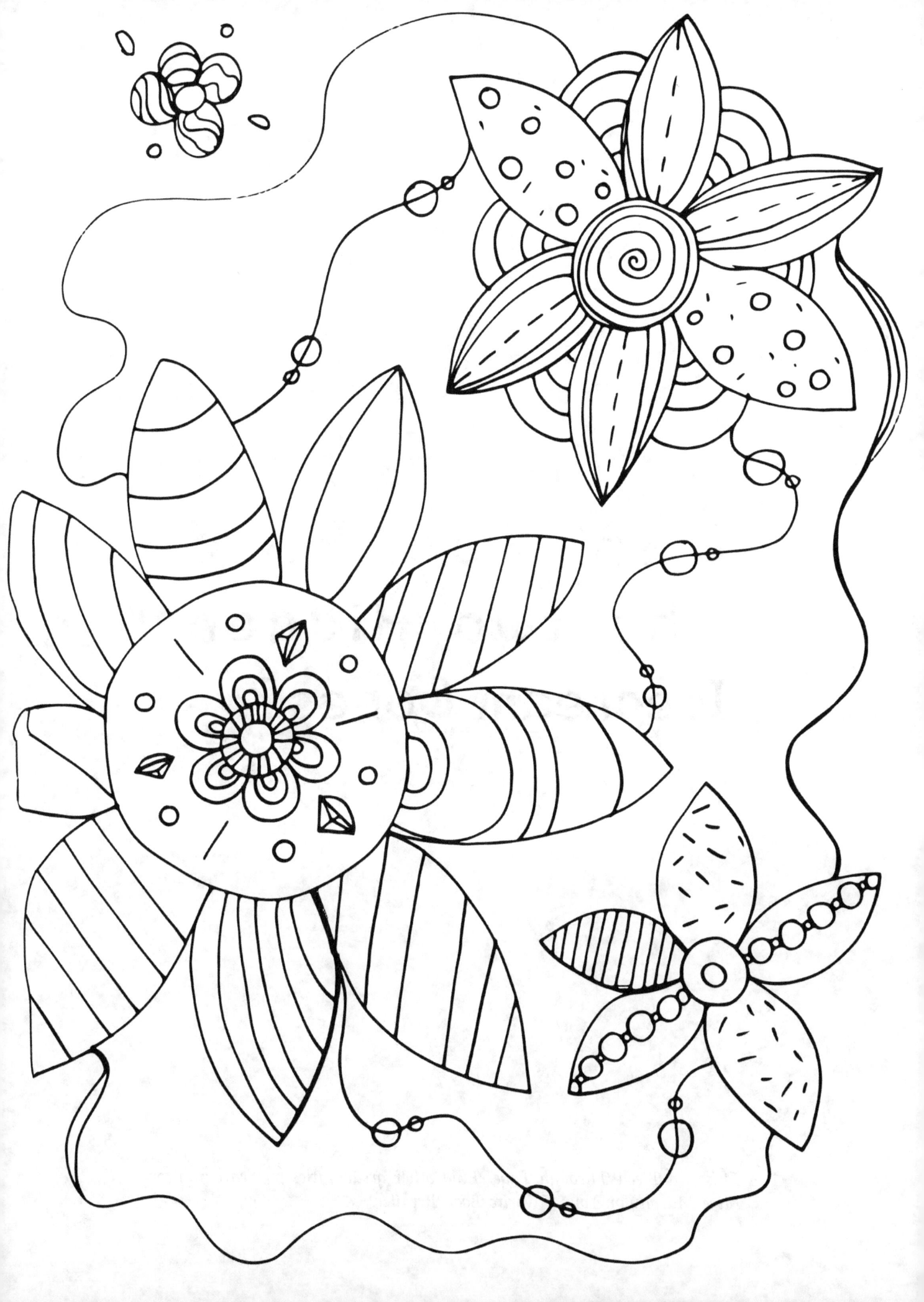

Can You Find The two Hidden Icecream Cones?

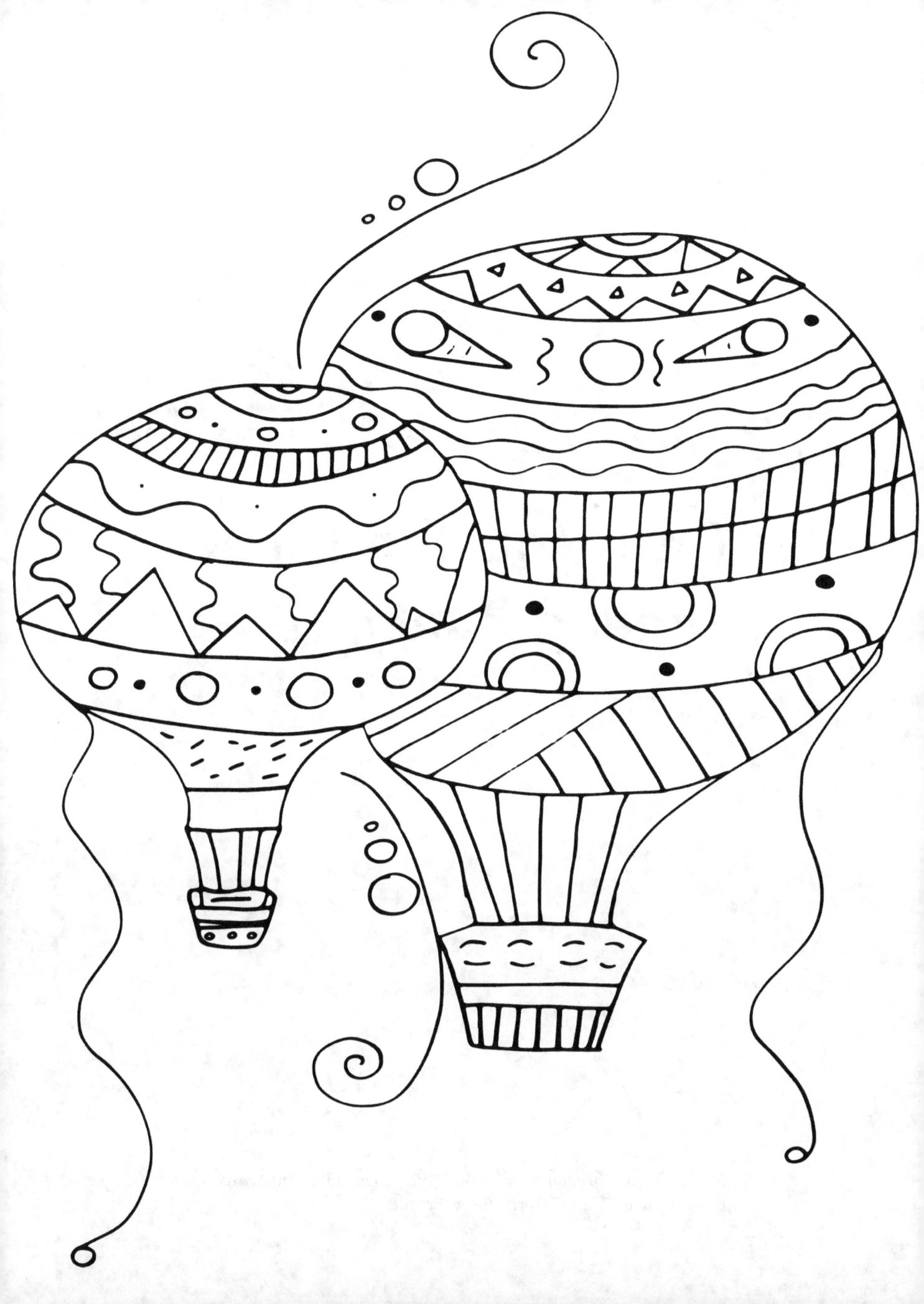

Can You Find The Hidden Eye?

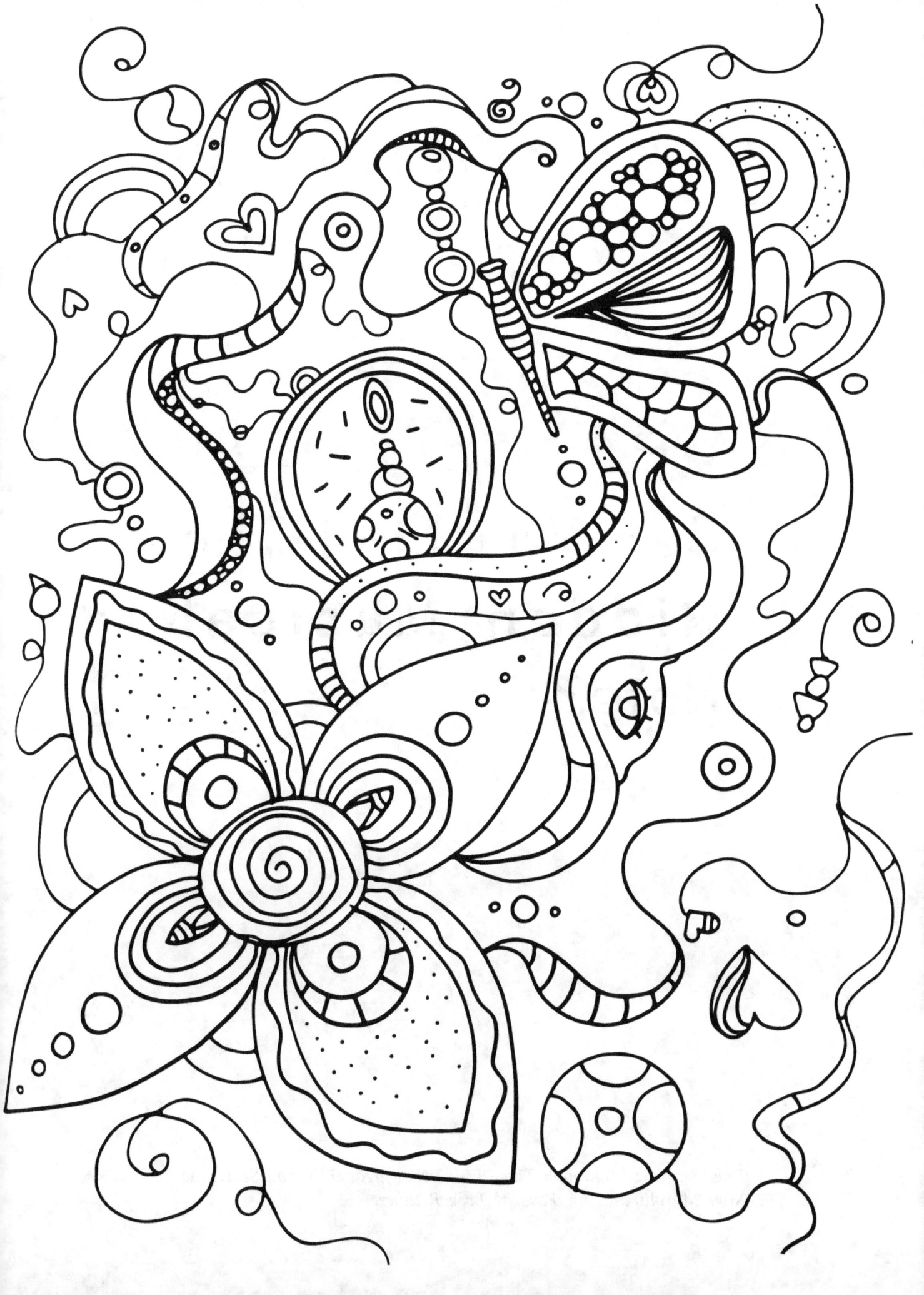

Can You Find The Hidden Musical Note?

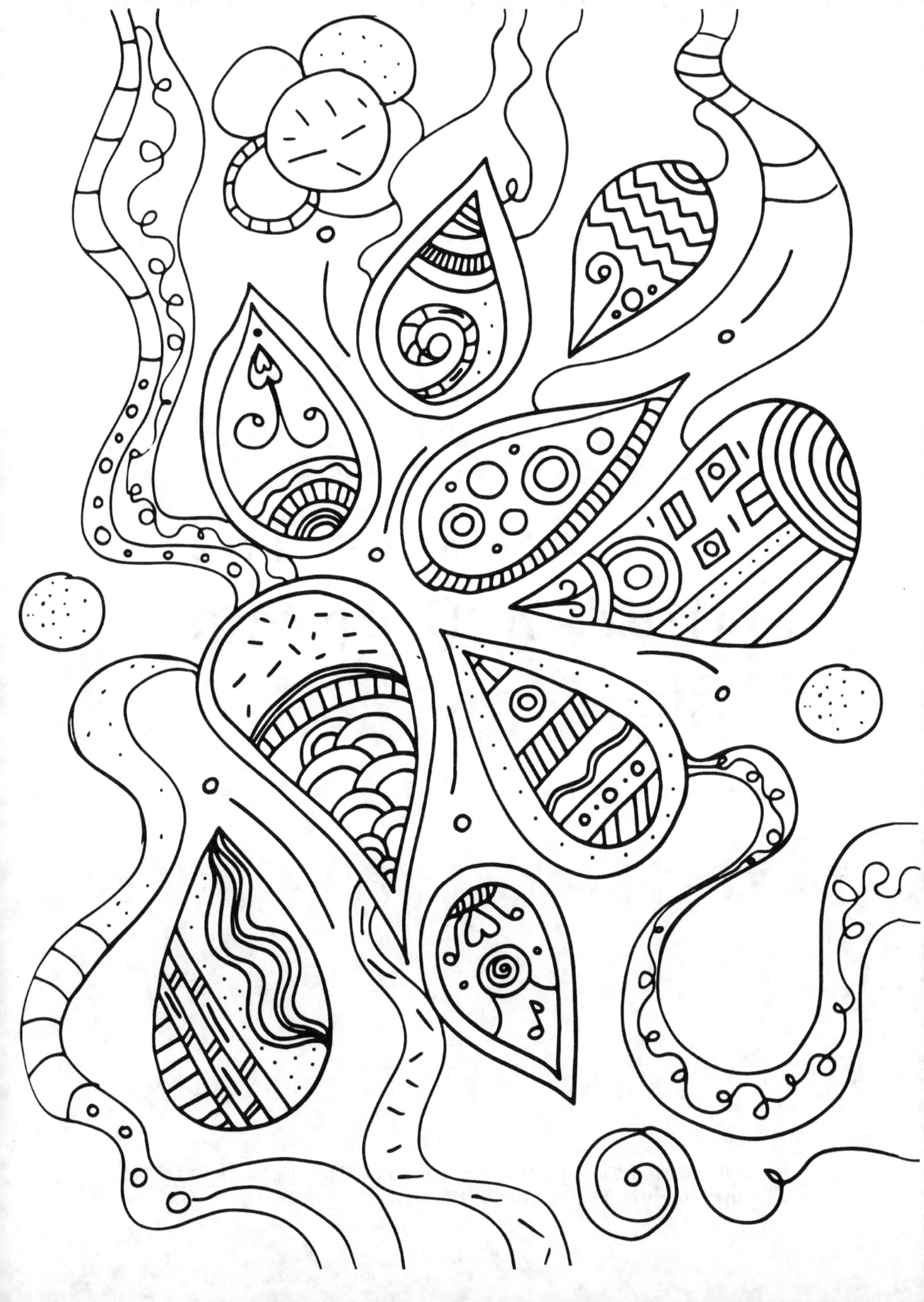

Can You Find The Hidden Diamond Ring?

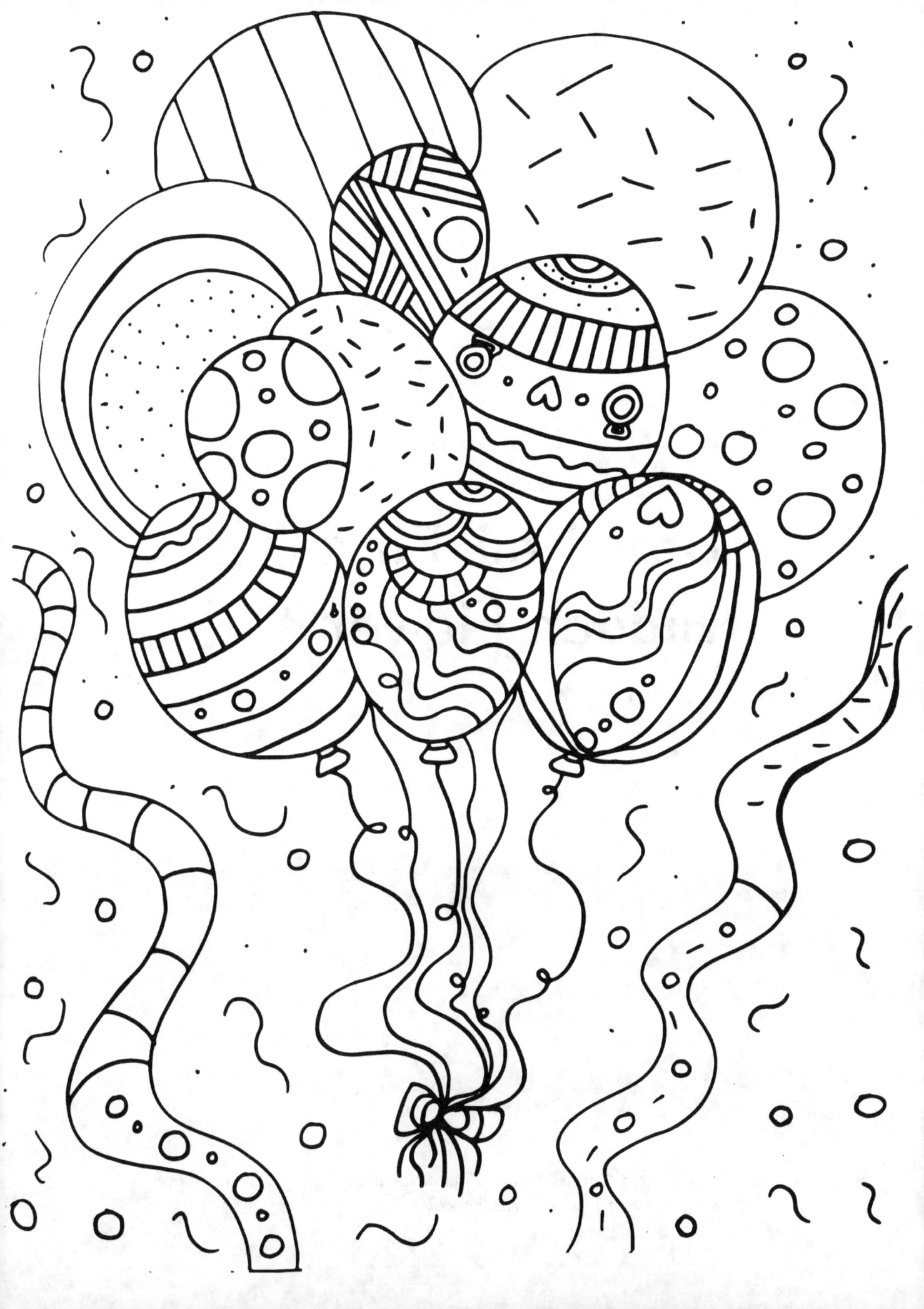

Can You Find The Hidden Flower?

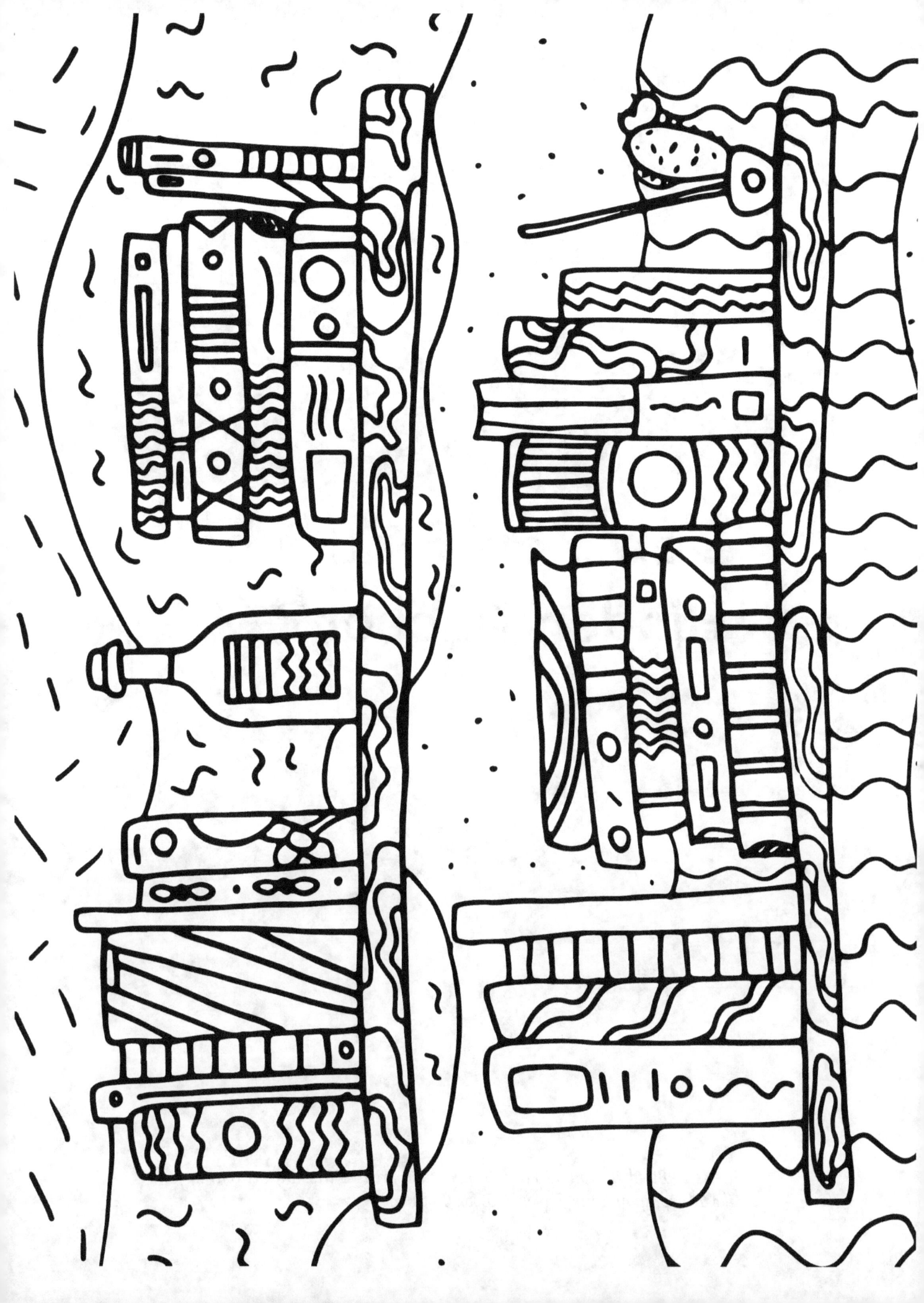

Can You Find The Hidden Anchor?

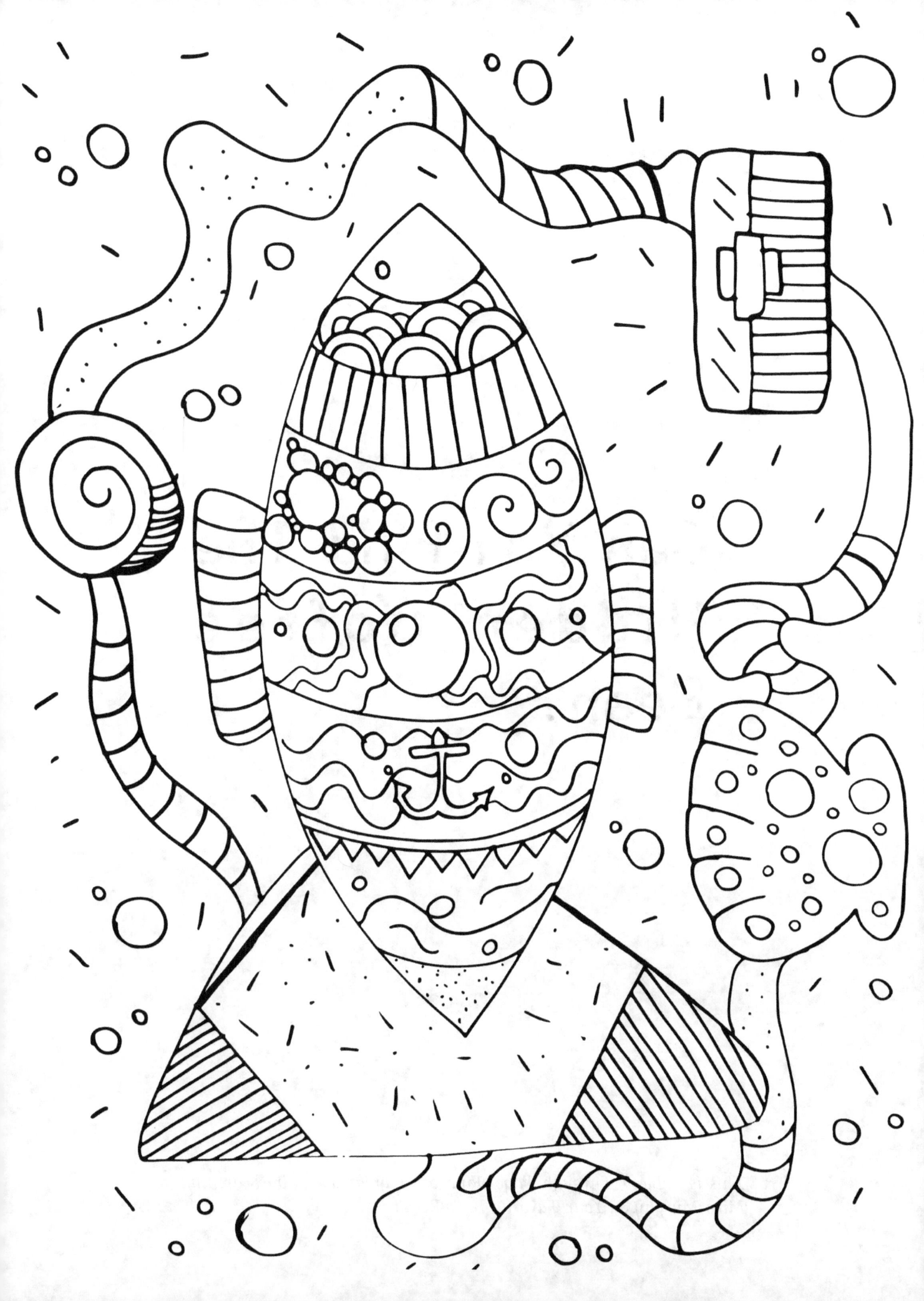

Can You Find The Hidden Coffee Bean?

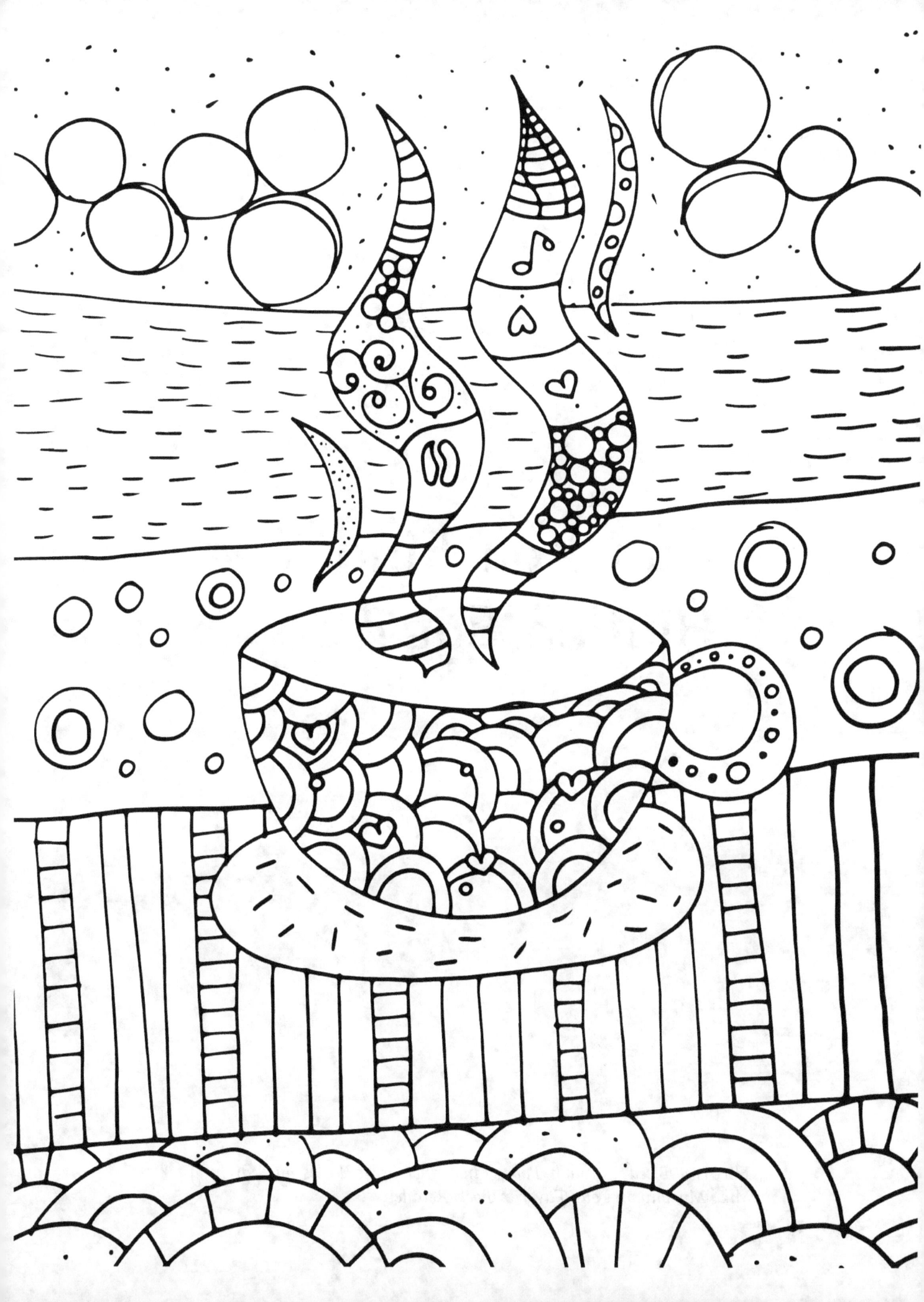

Can You Find The Hidden Eye?

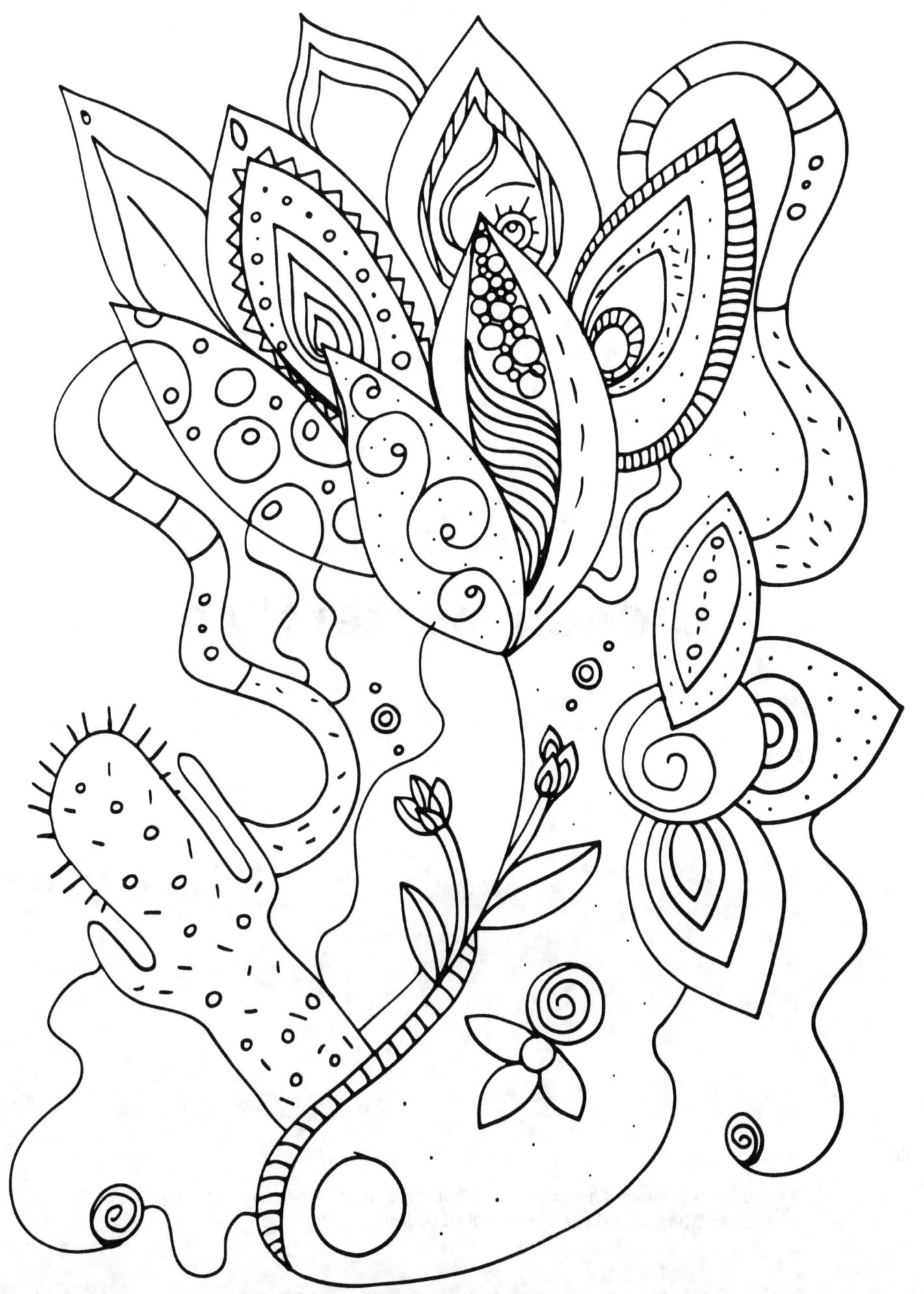

Can You Find The Hidden Butterfly?

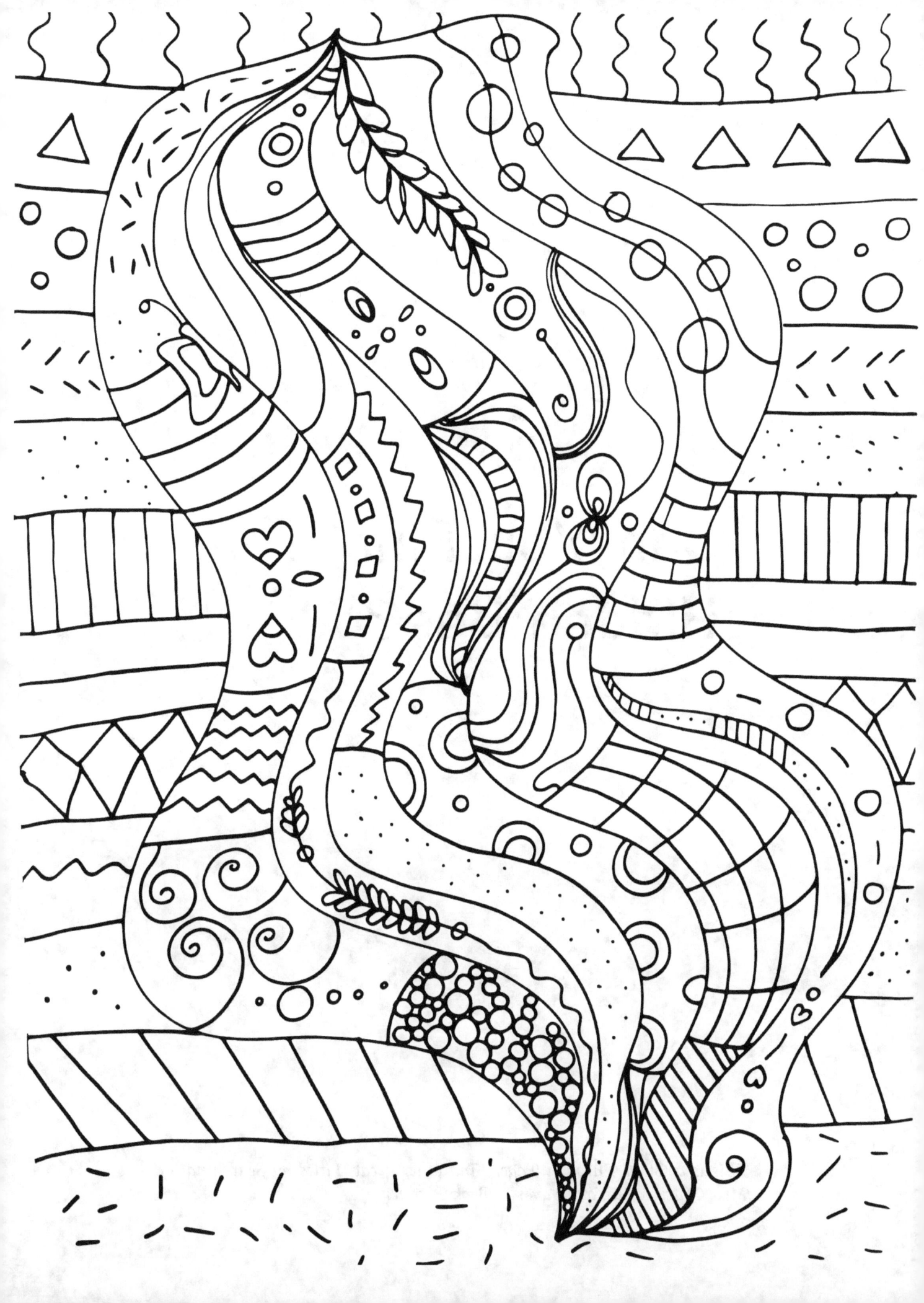

Can You Find The Hidden Bee?

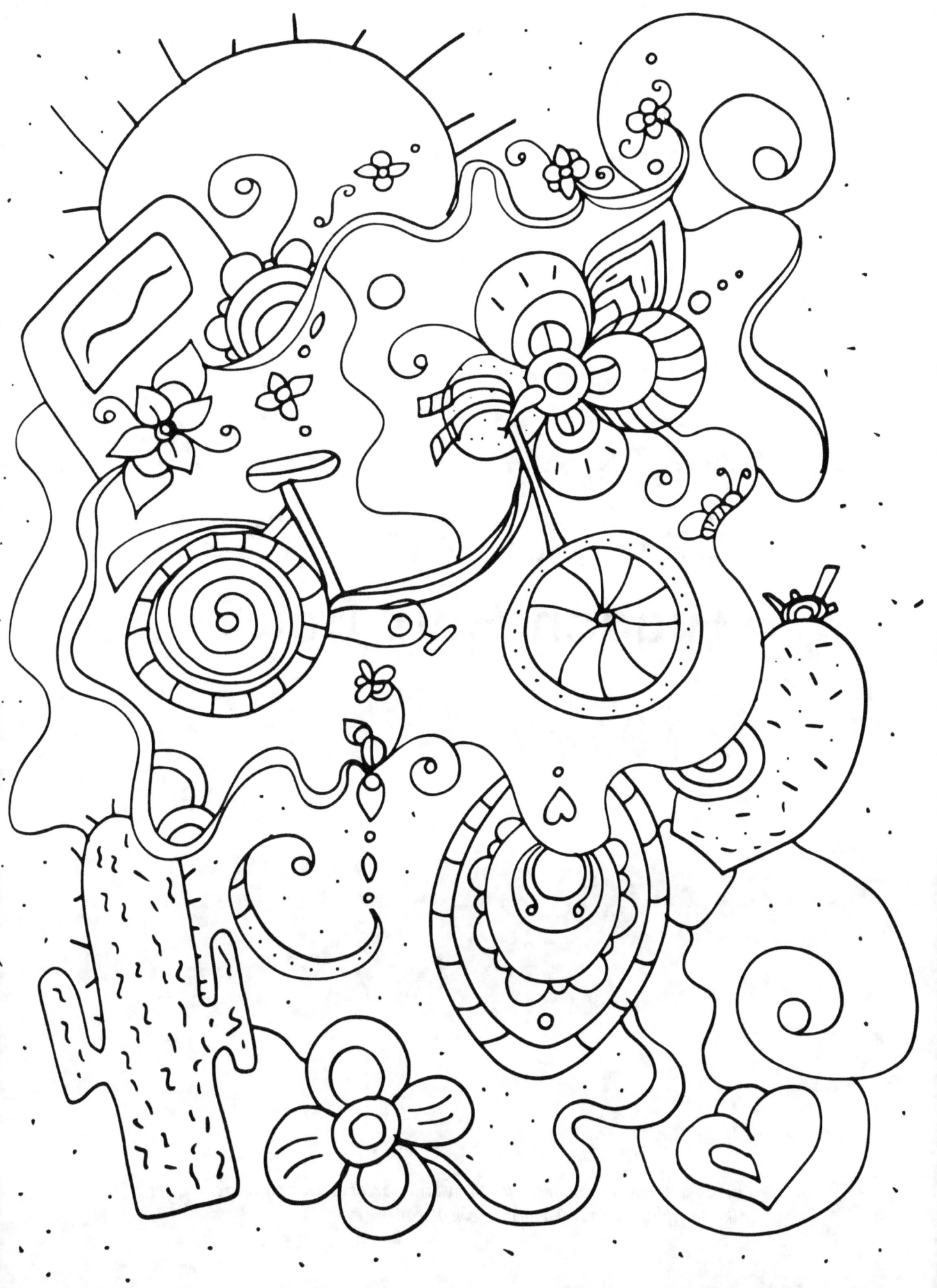

Can You Find The Hidden Hair Bow?

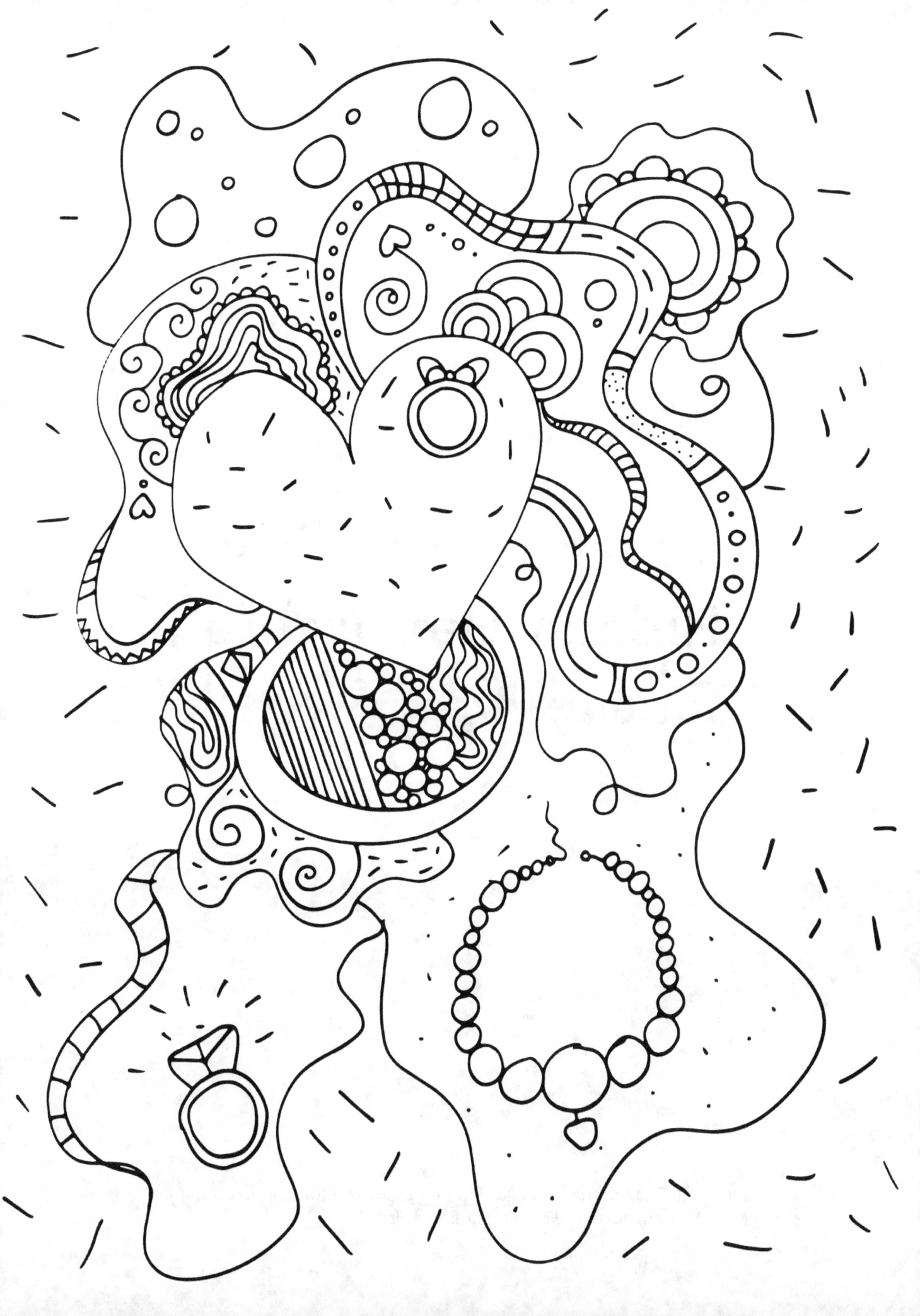

Can You Find The Hidden Hat with a Flower?

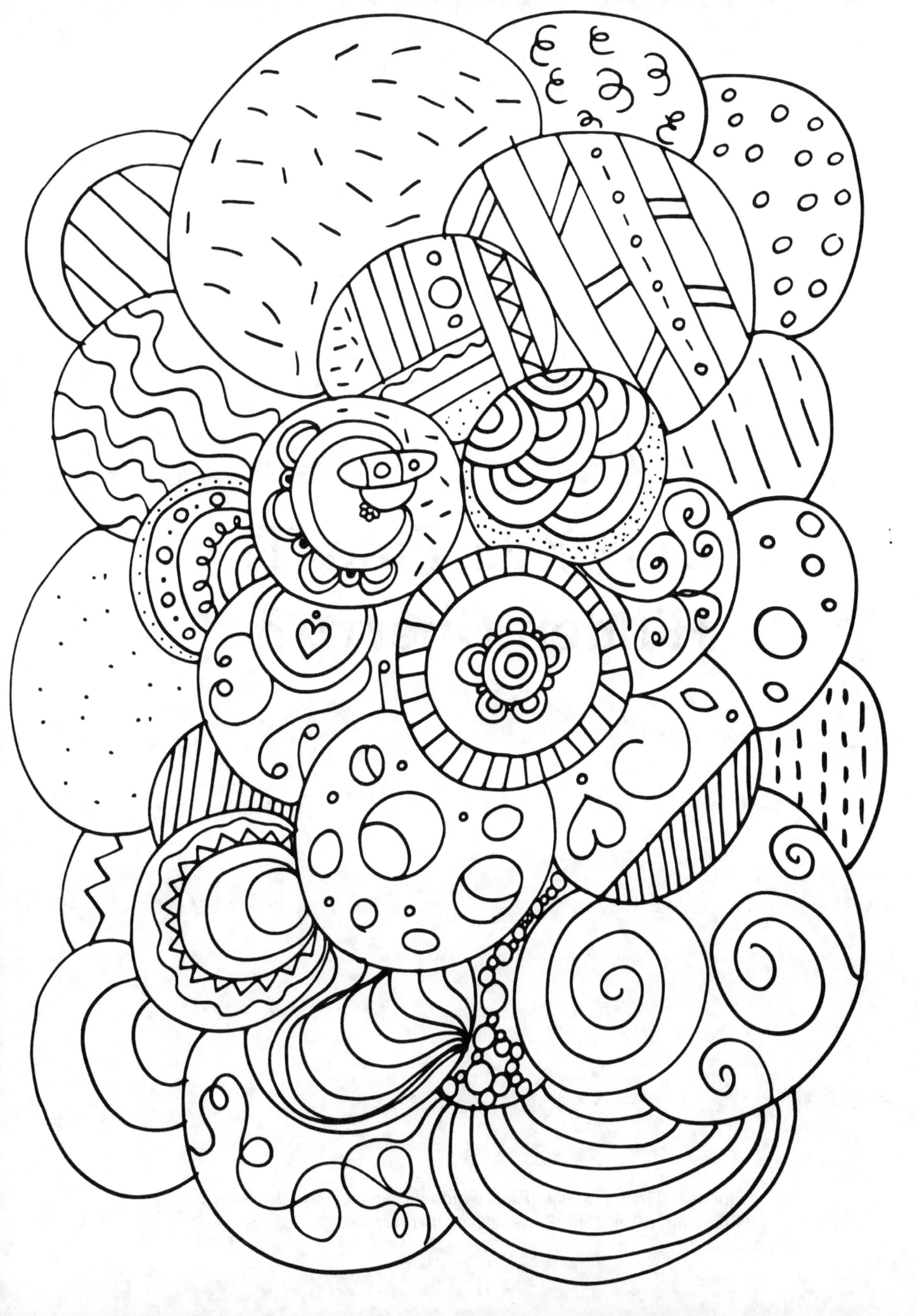

Can You Find The Hidden Cherry?

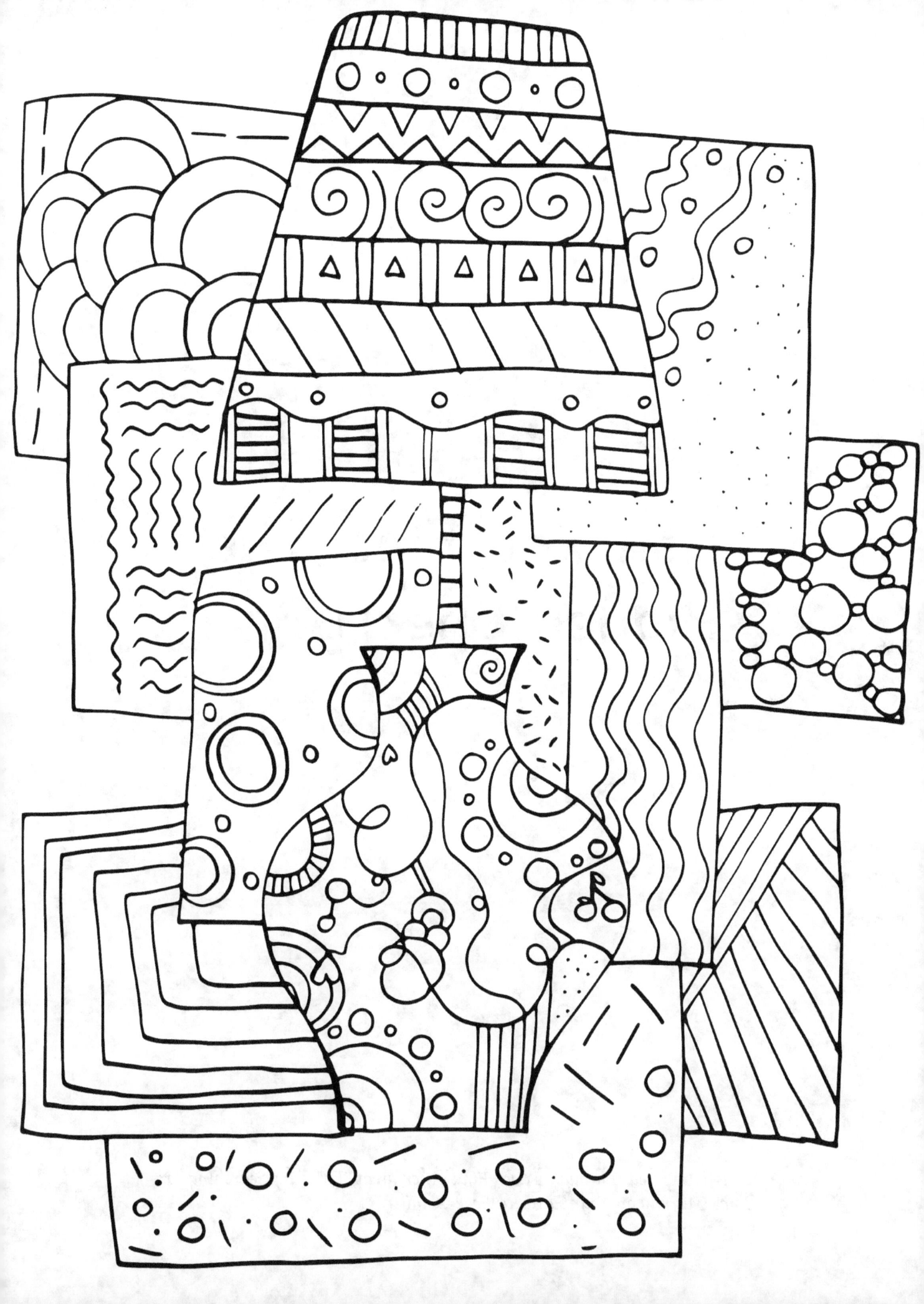

Can You Find The Hidden Cherry?

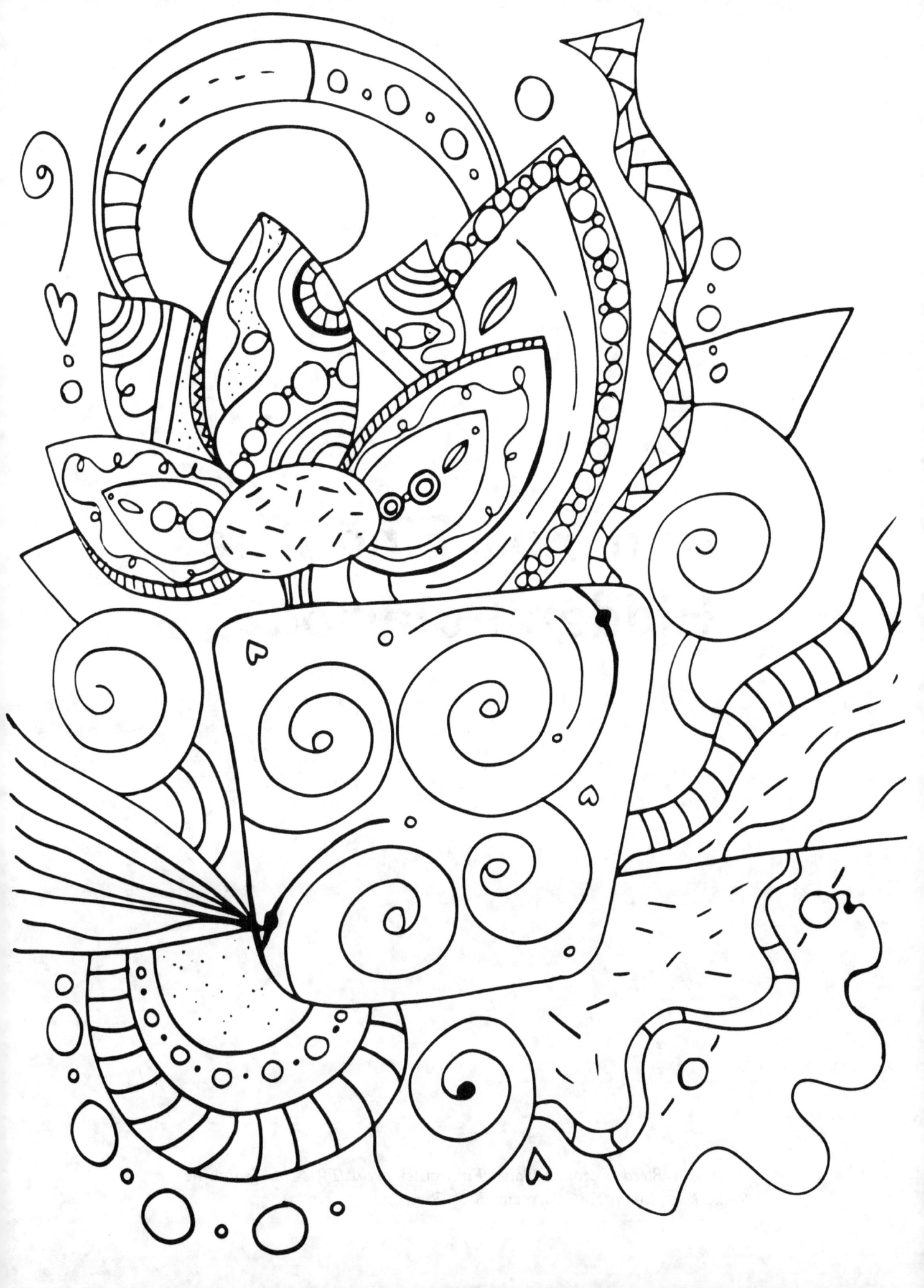

Can You Find The Hidden Polariod?

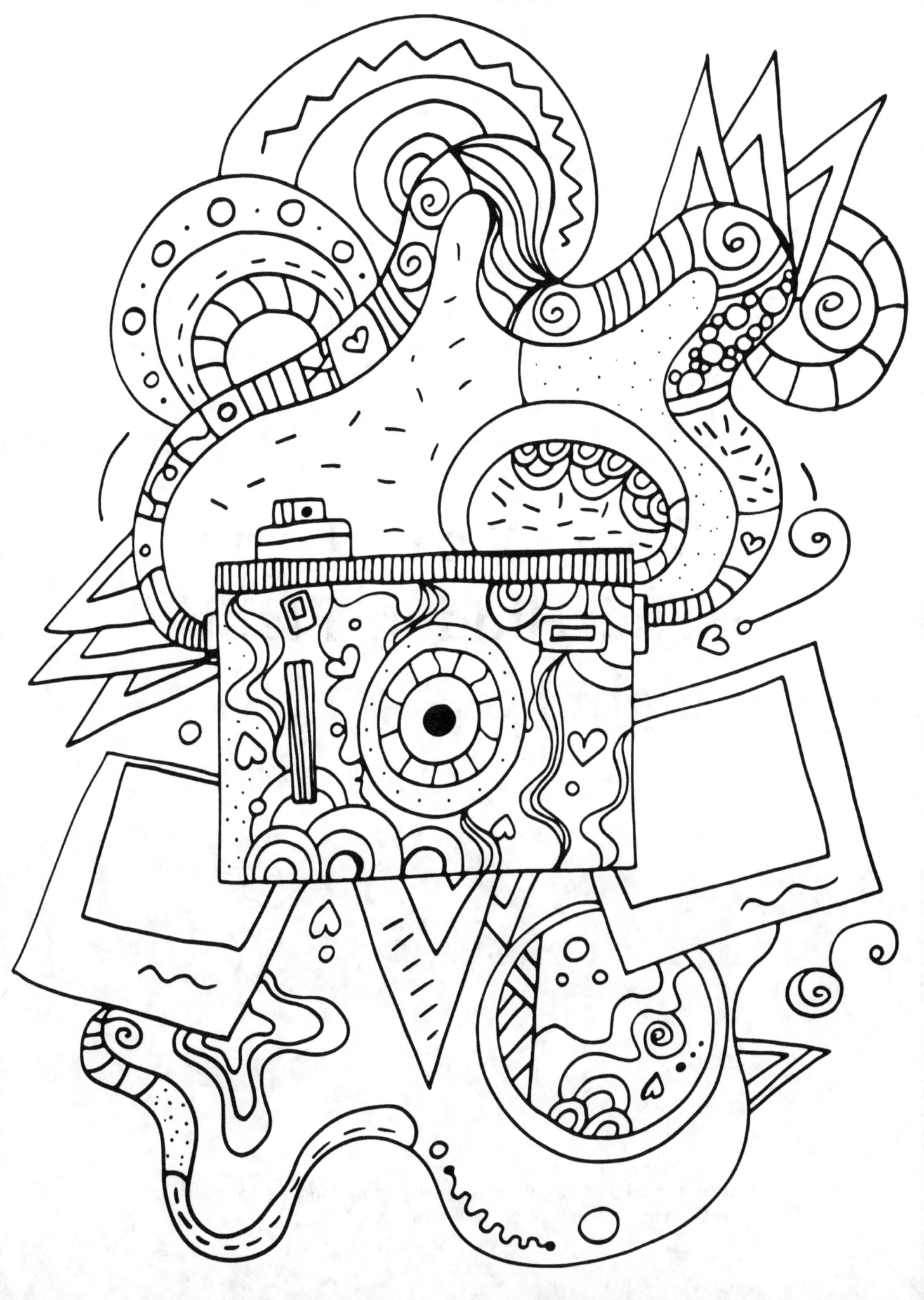

Can You Find The Hidden Flash Light?

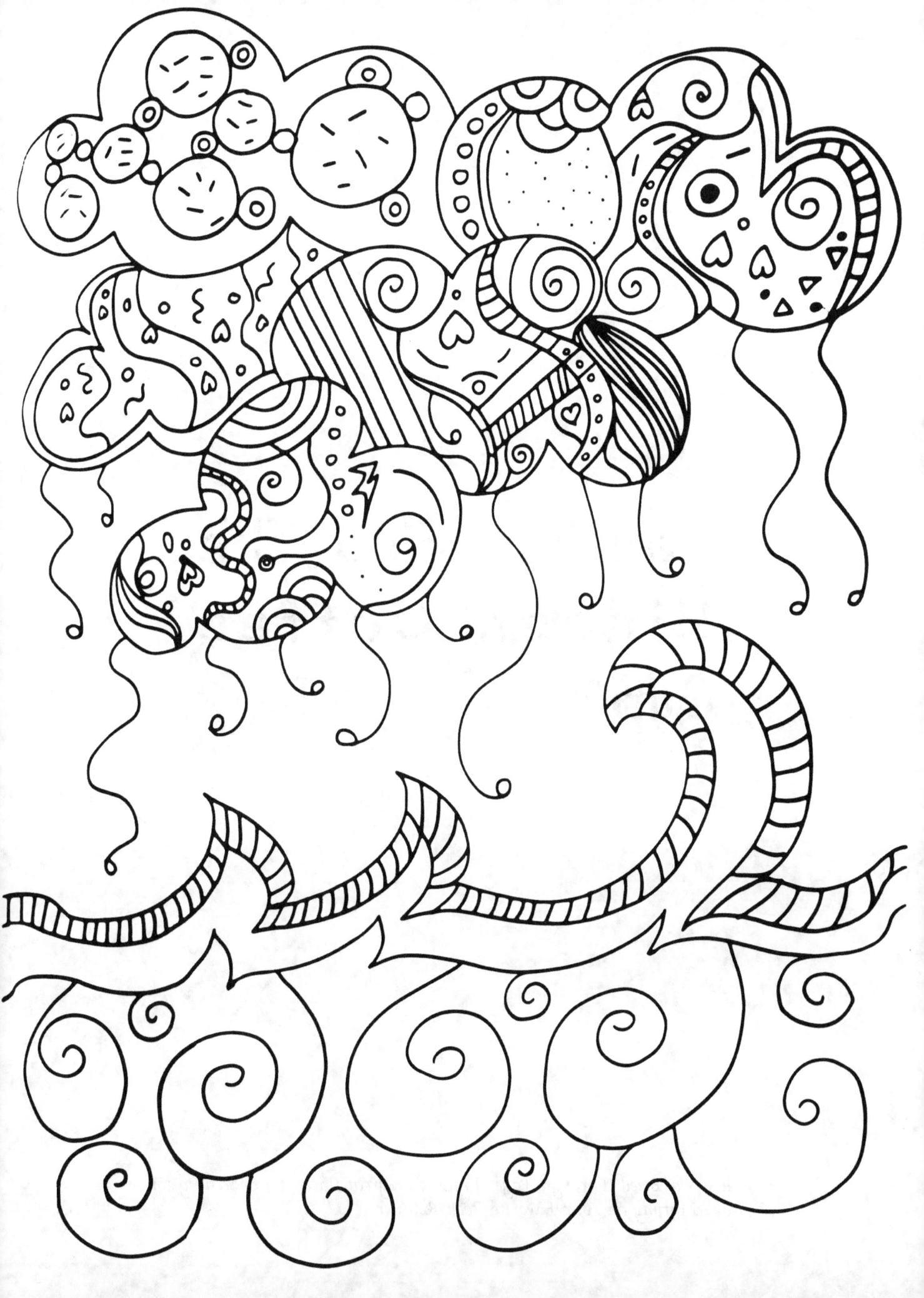

Can You Find The Hidden Coffee Cup?

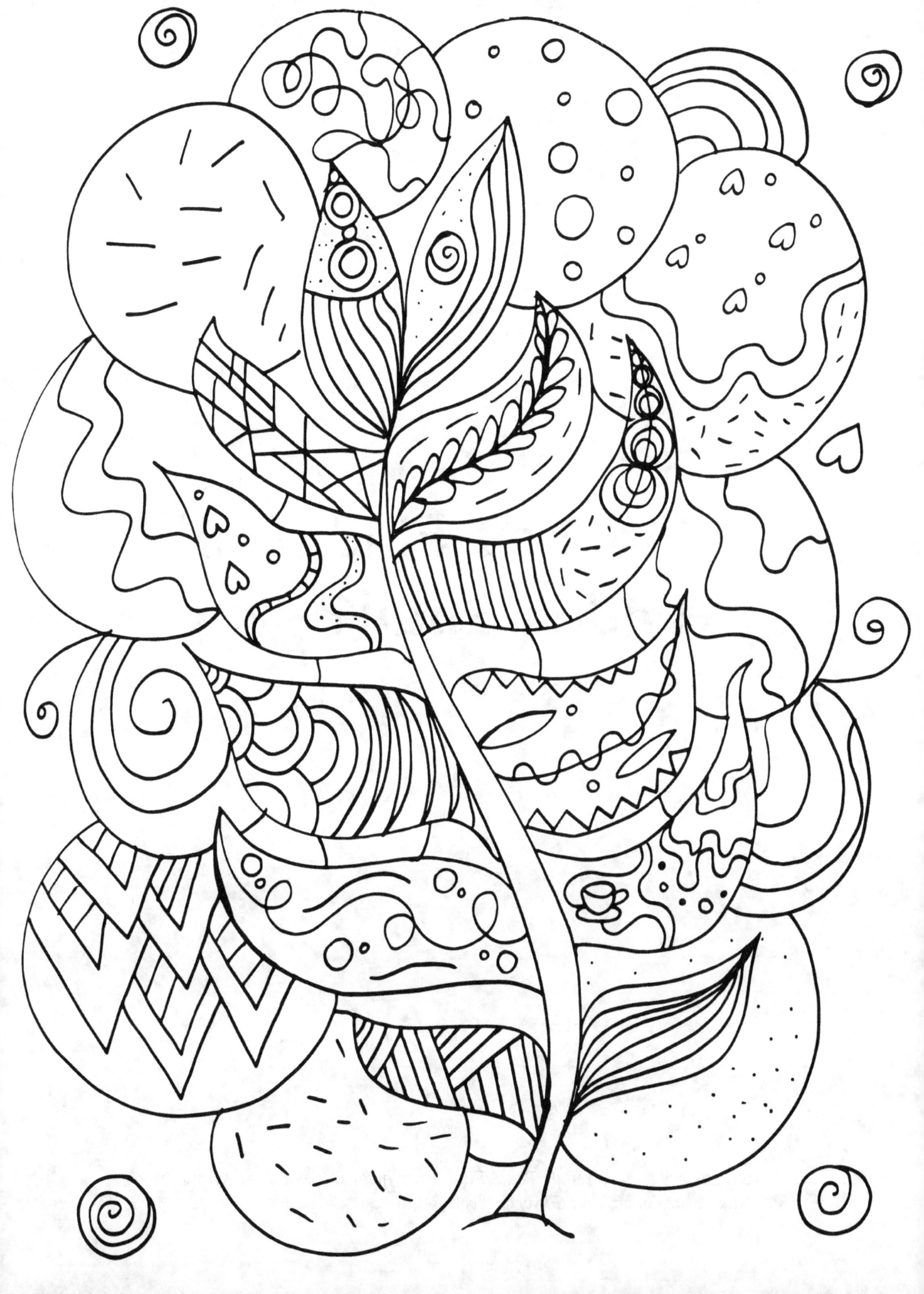

Can You Find The Hidden Snail?

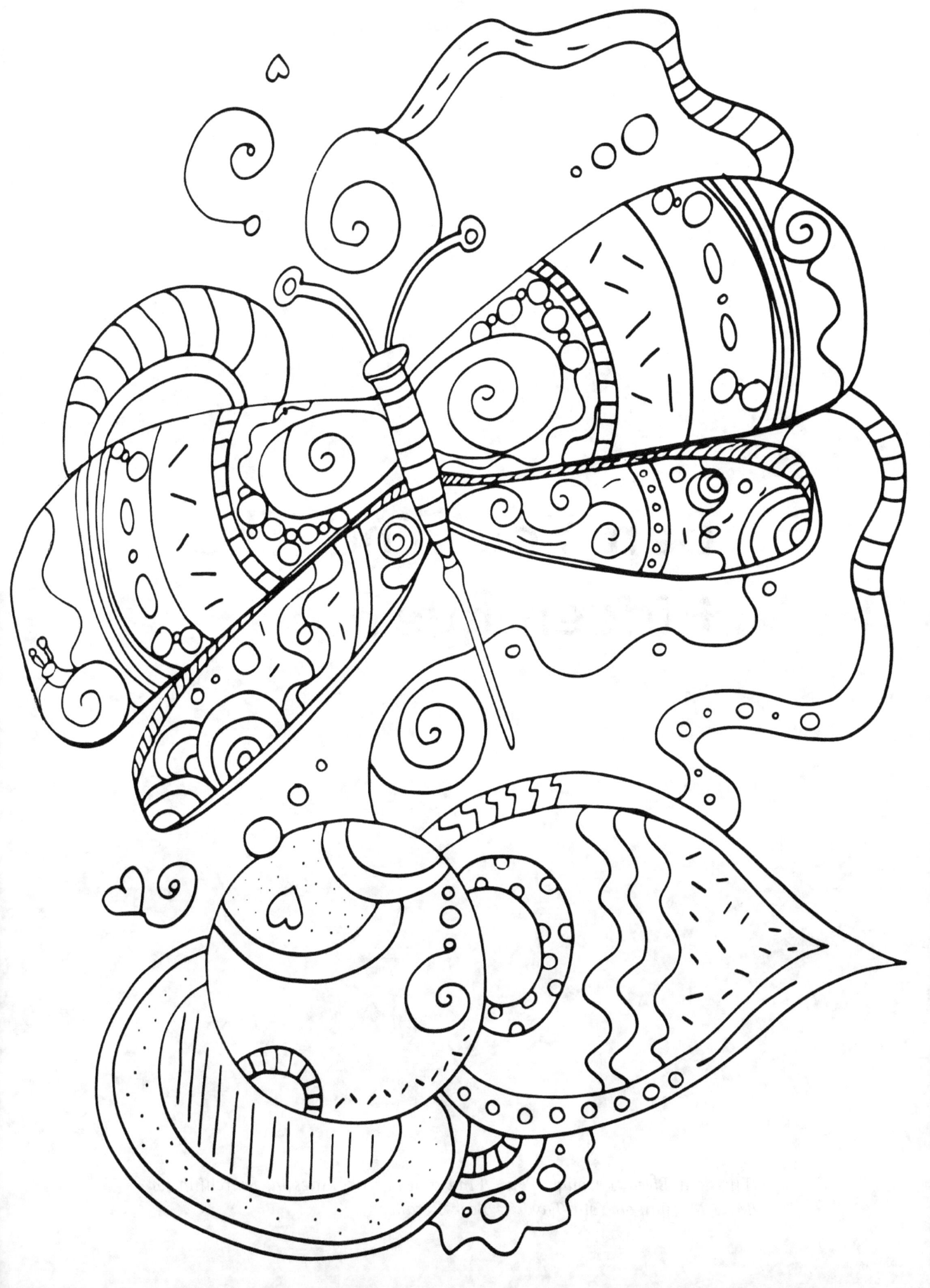

Can You Find The Hidden Eye?

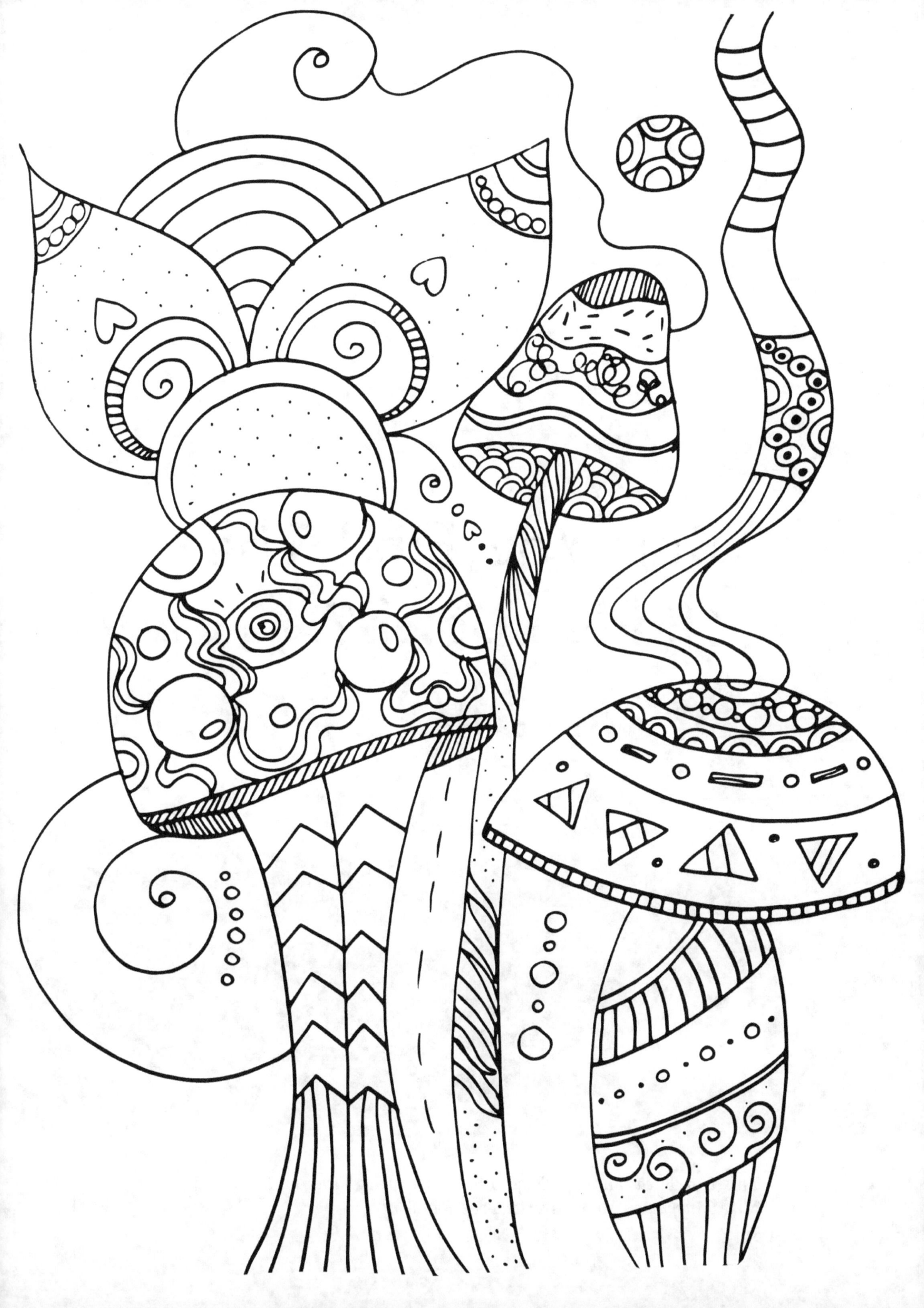

Can You Find The Hidden Comb?

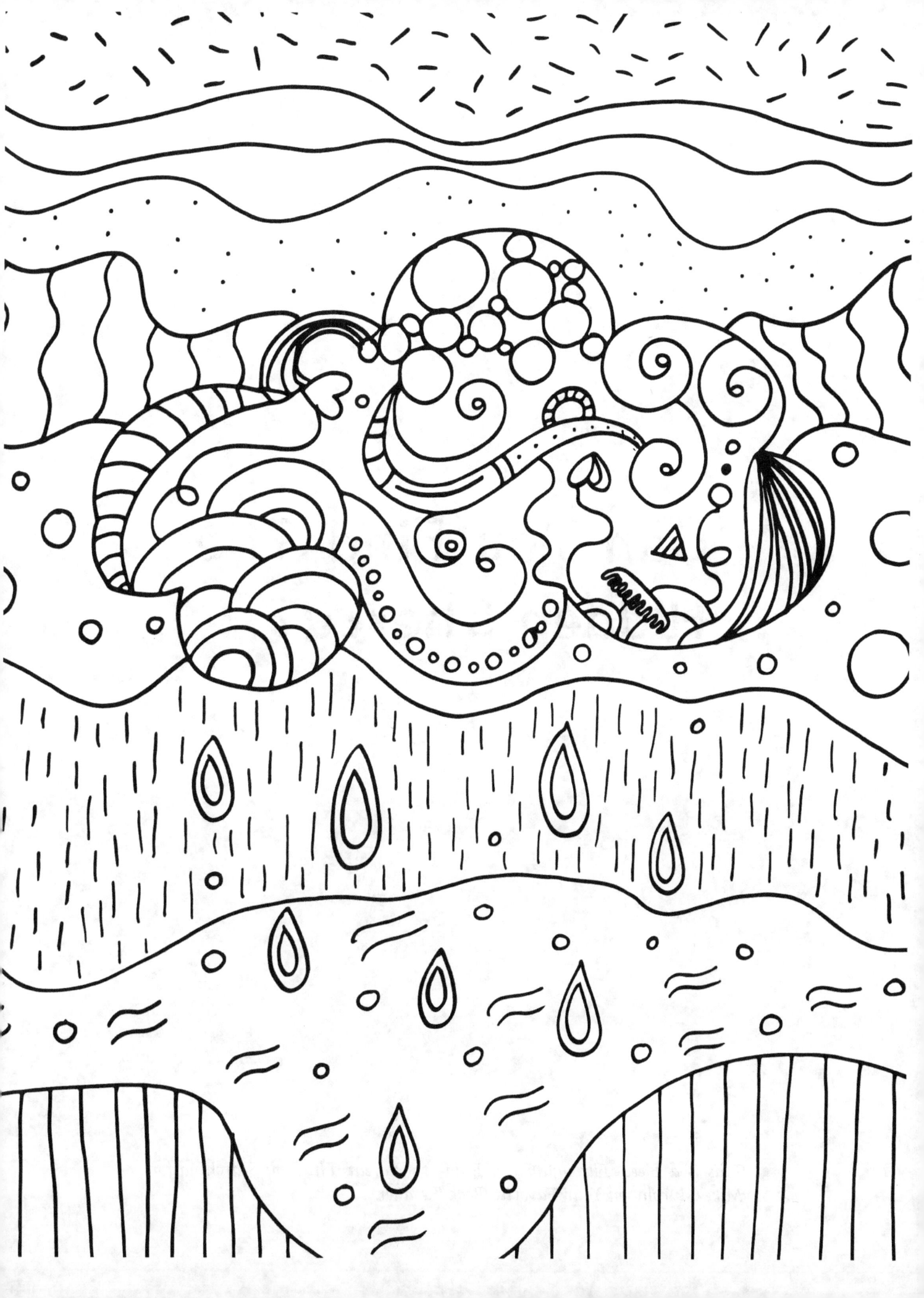

Can You Find The Hidden Cherry?

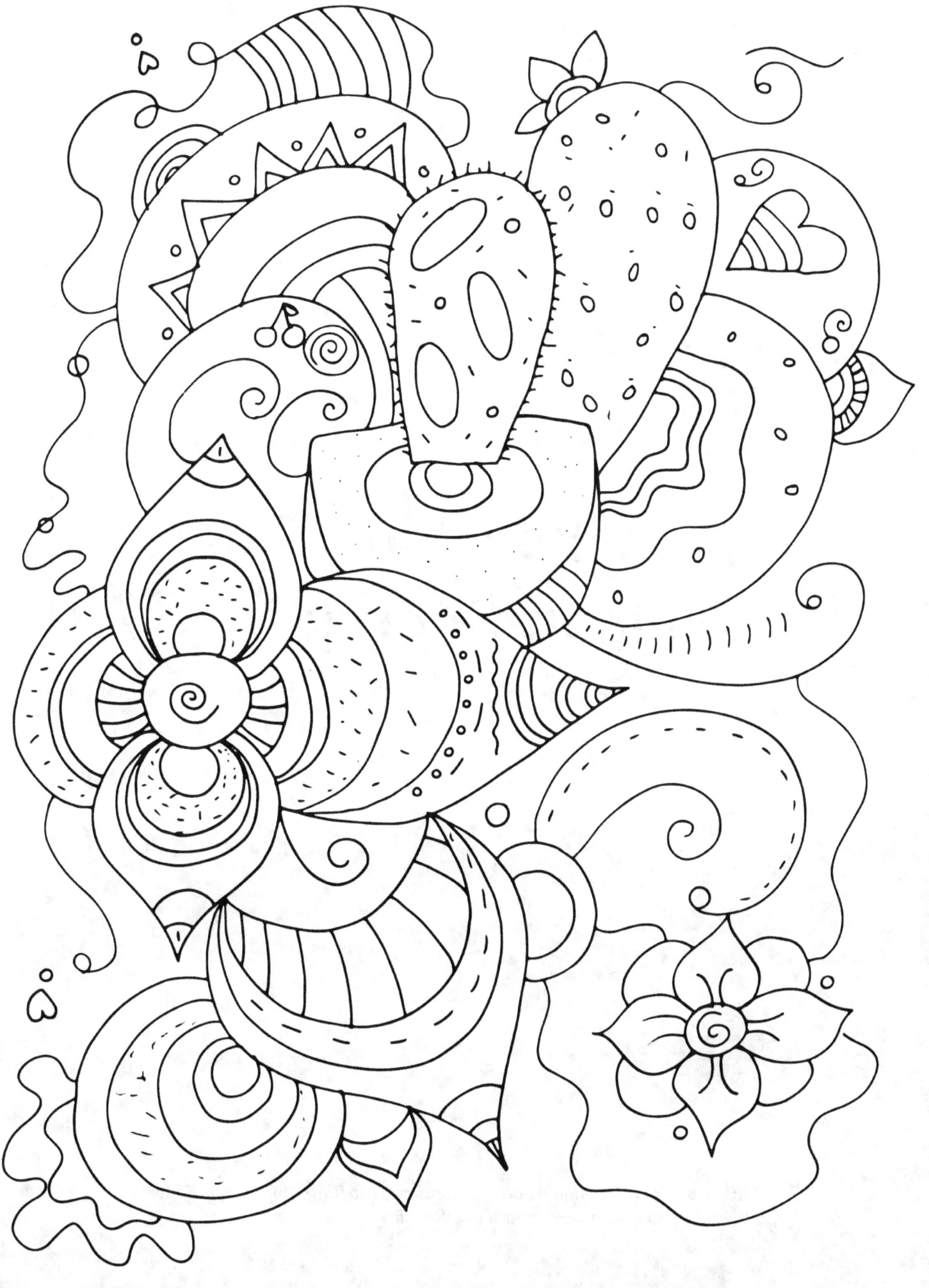

Can You Find The Hidden Cherry?

Can You Find The Hidden Diamond Ring?

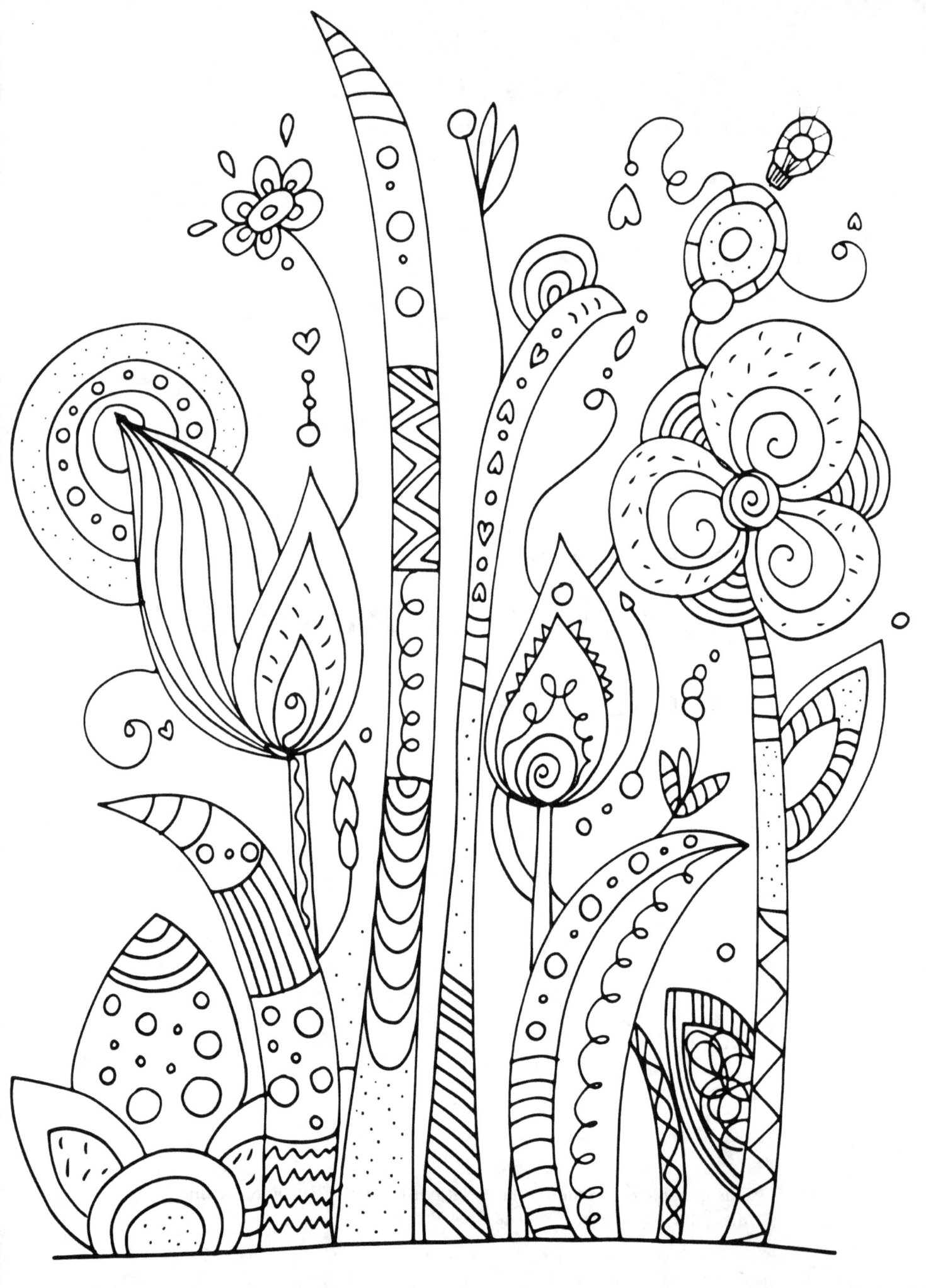

Can You Find The Hidden Bulb?

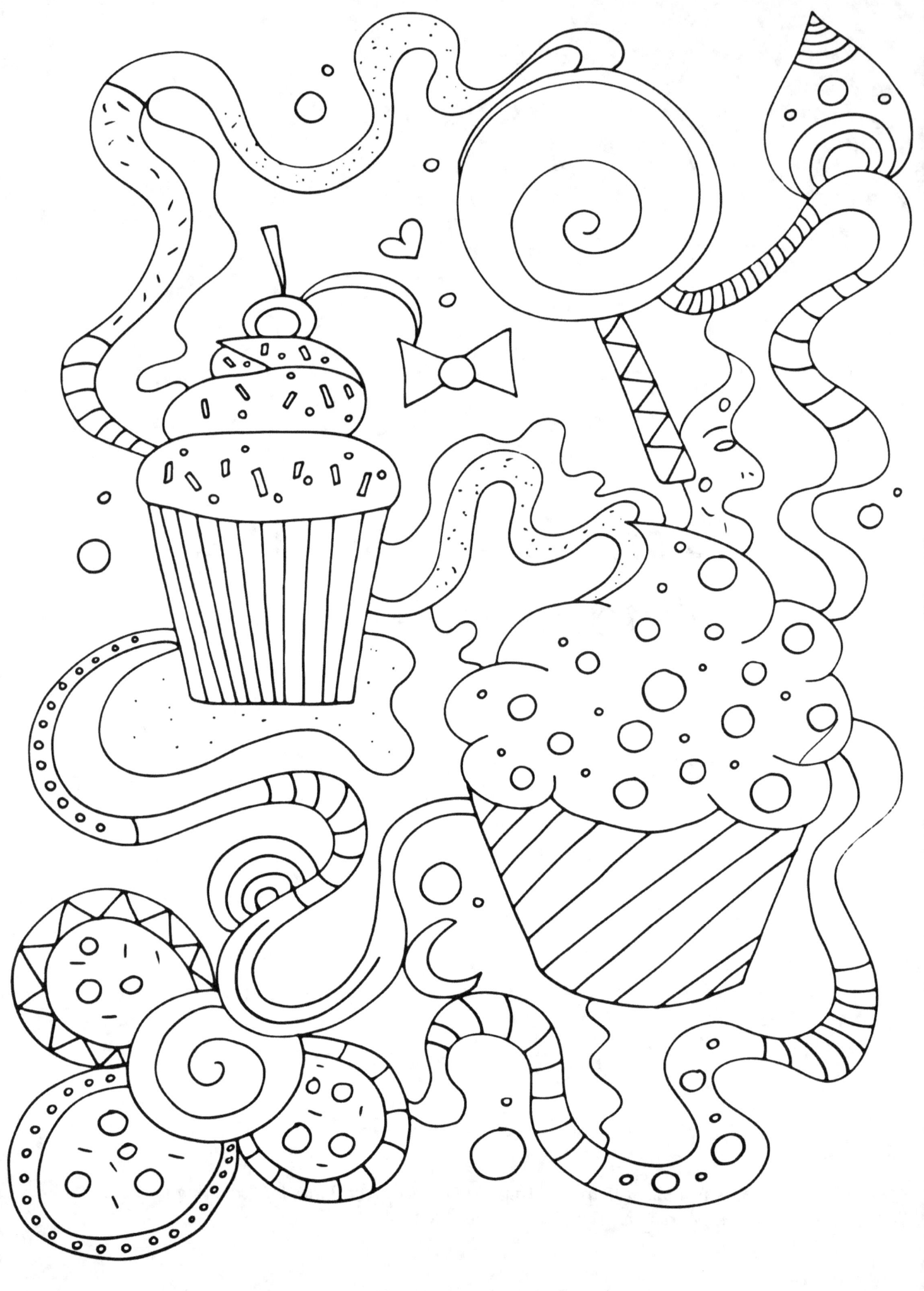

Can You Find The Hidden Shape Of Moon?

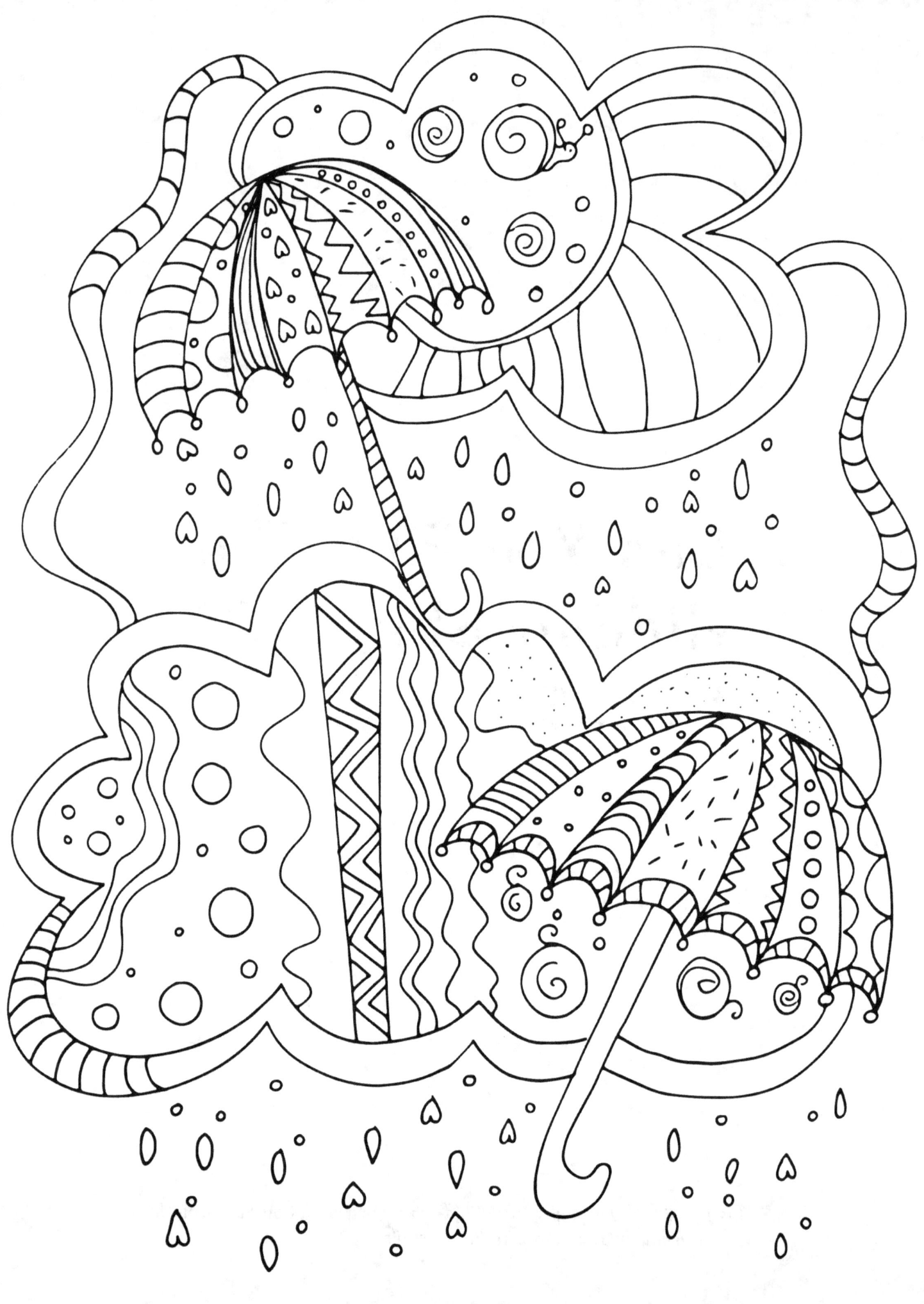

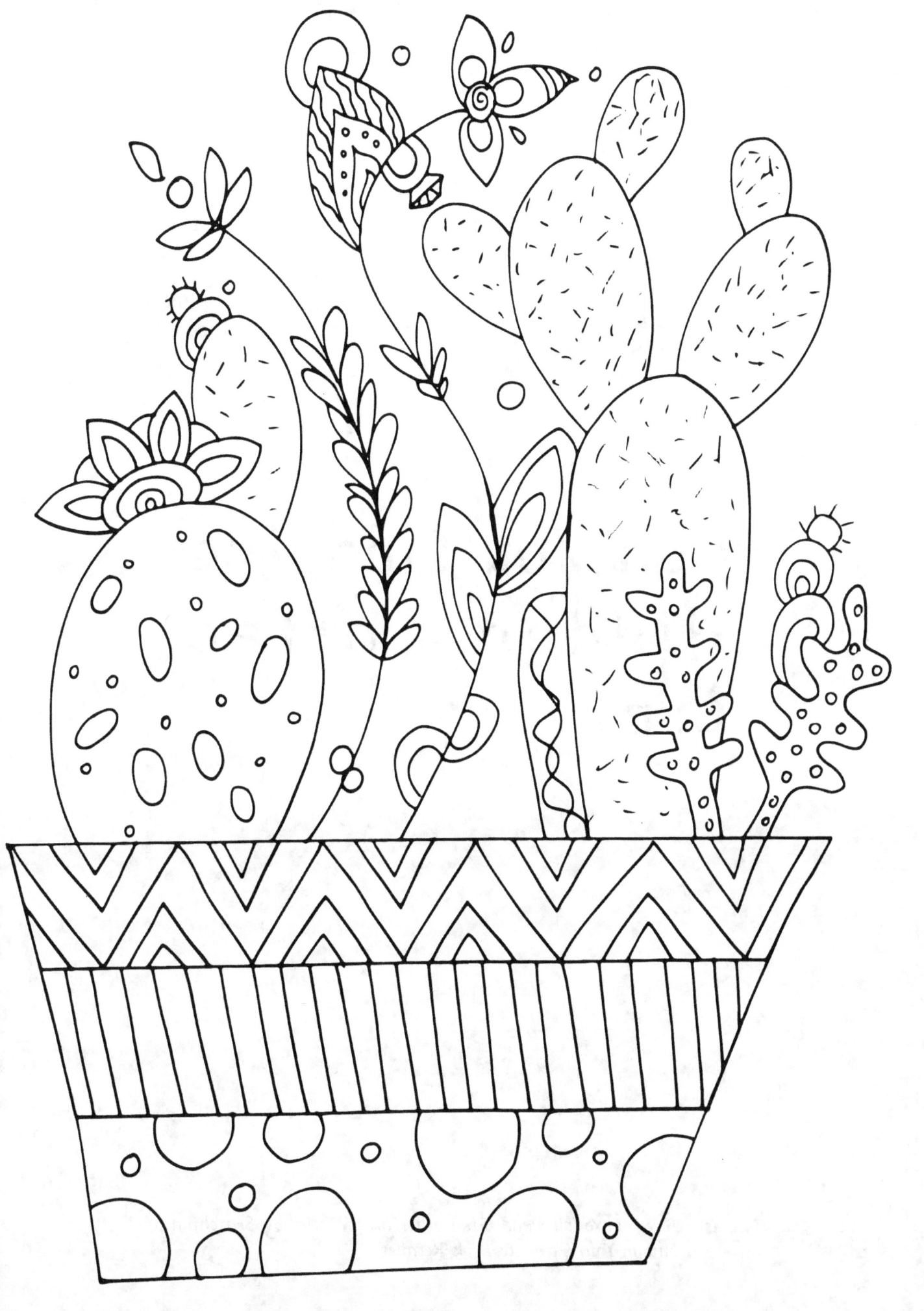

Can You Find The Hidden Coffee Cup?

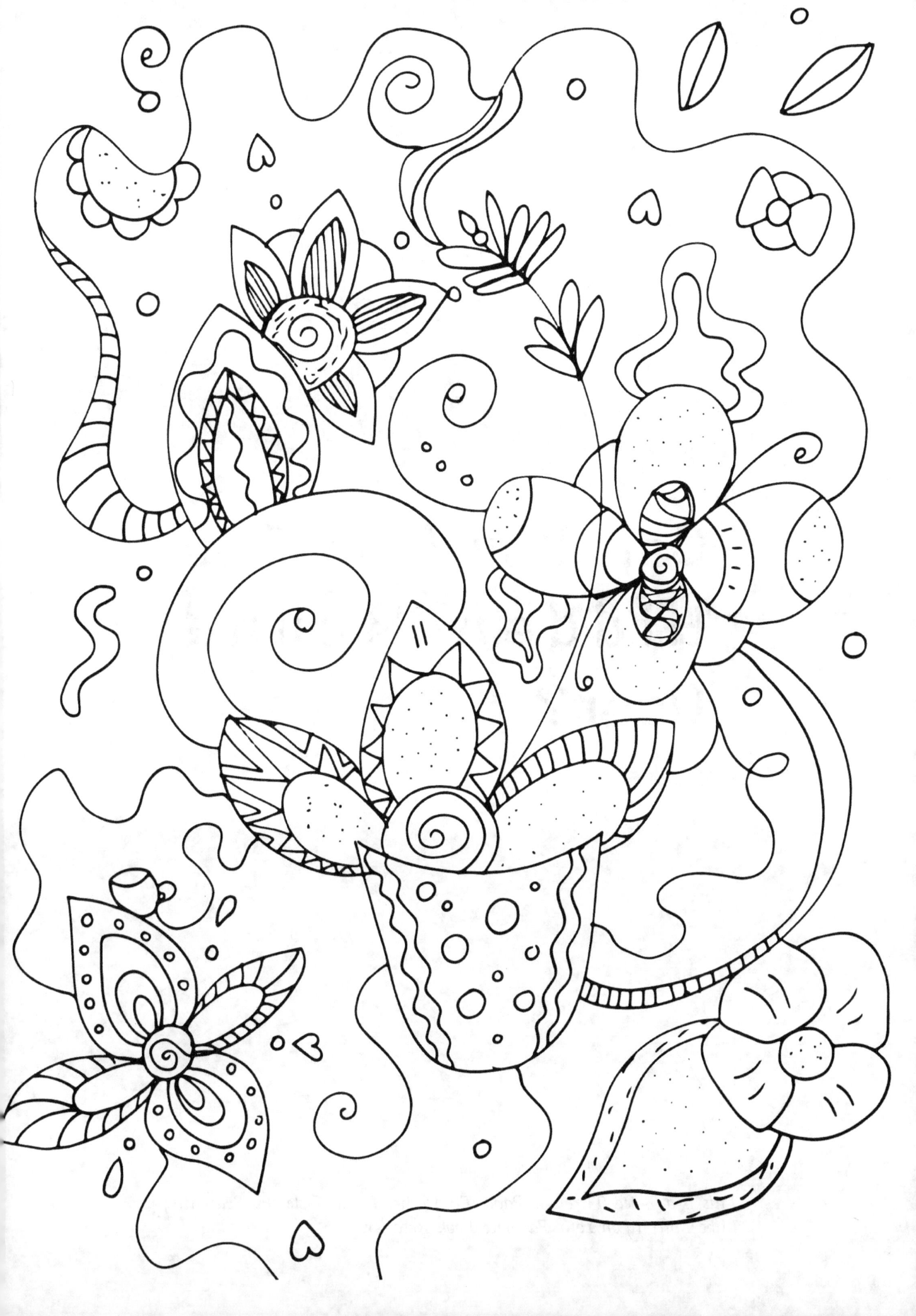

Can You Find The Hidden Round Door?

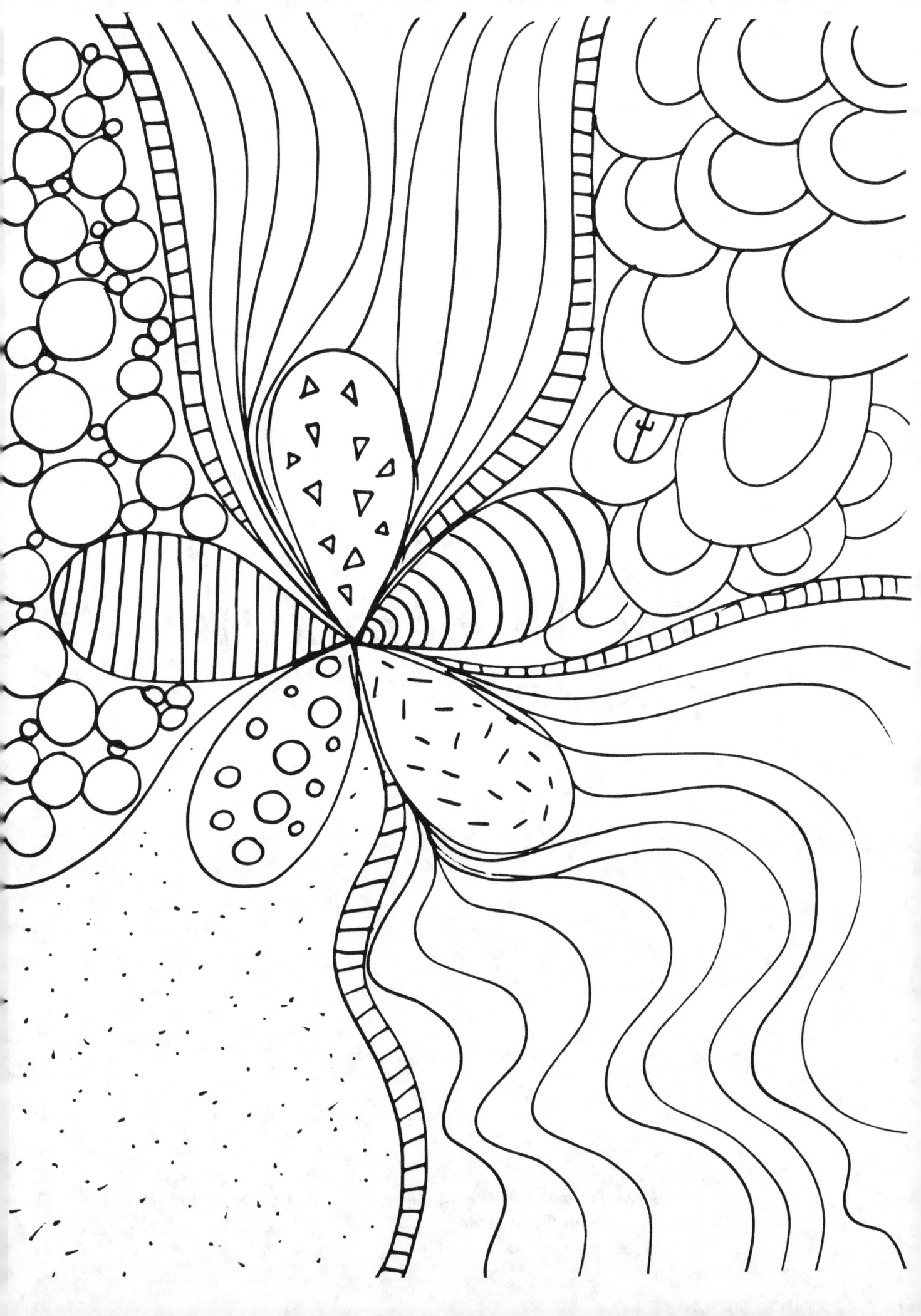

Can You Find
The Hidden Little
Cloud?

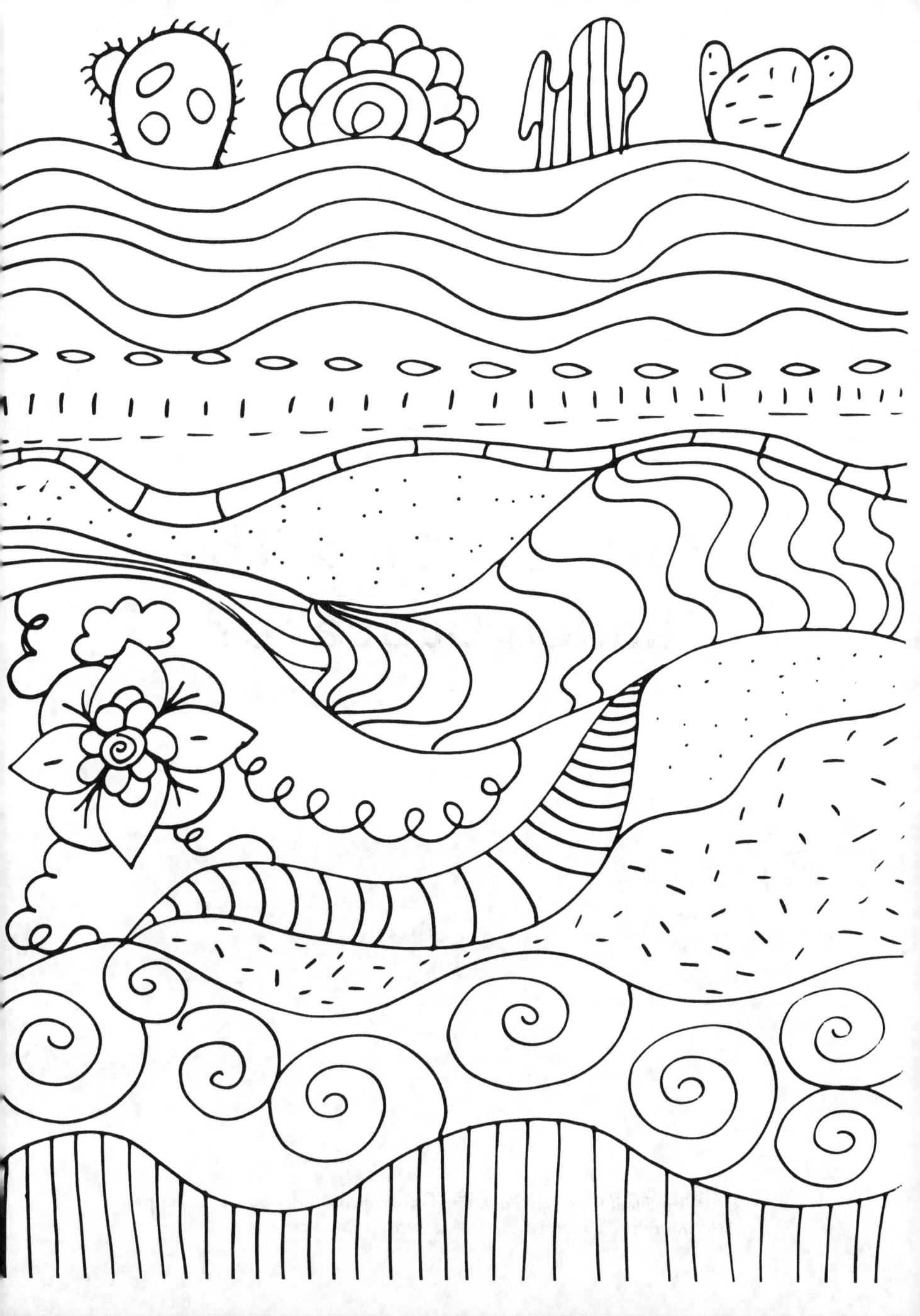

Can You Find The Hidden Cupcake?

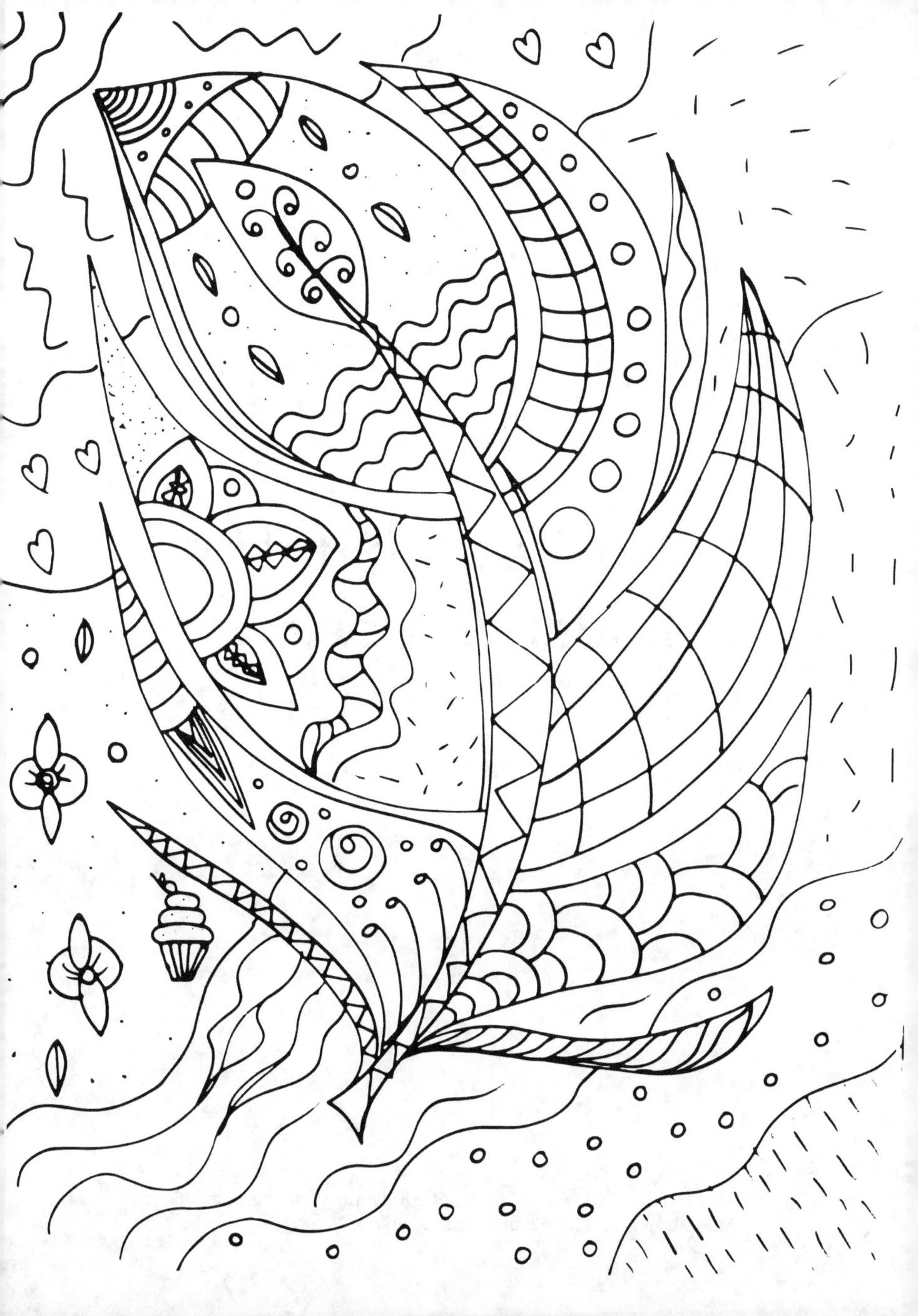

Can You Find The Hidden Grape?

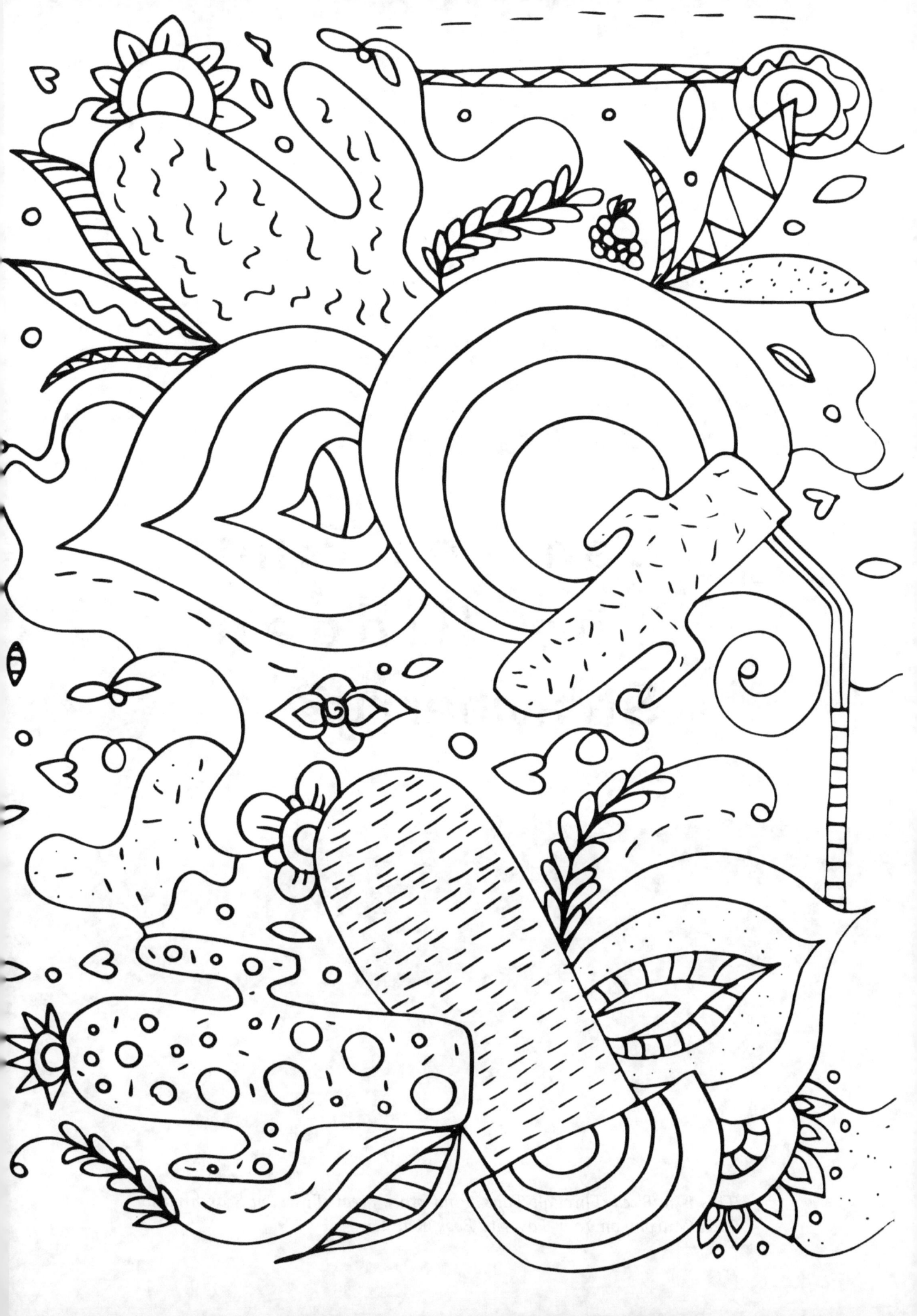

Can You Find The Hidden Strawberry?

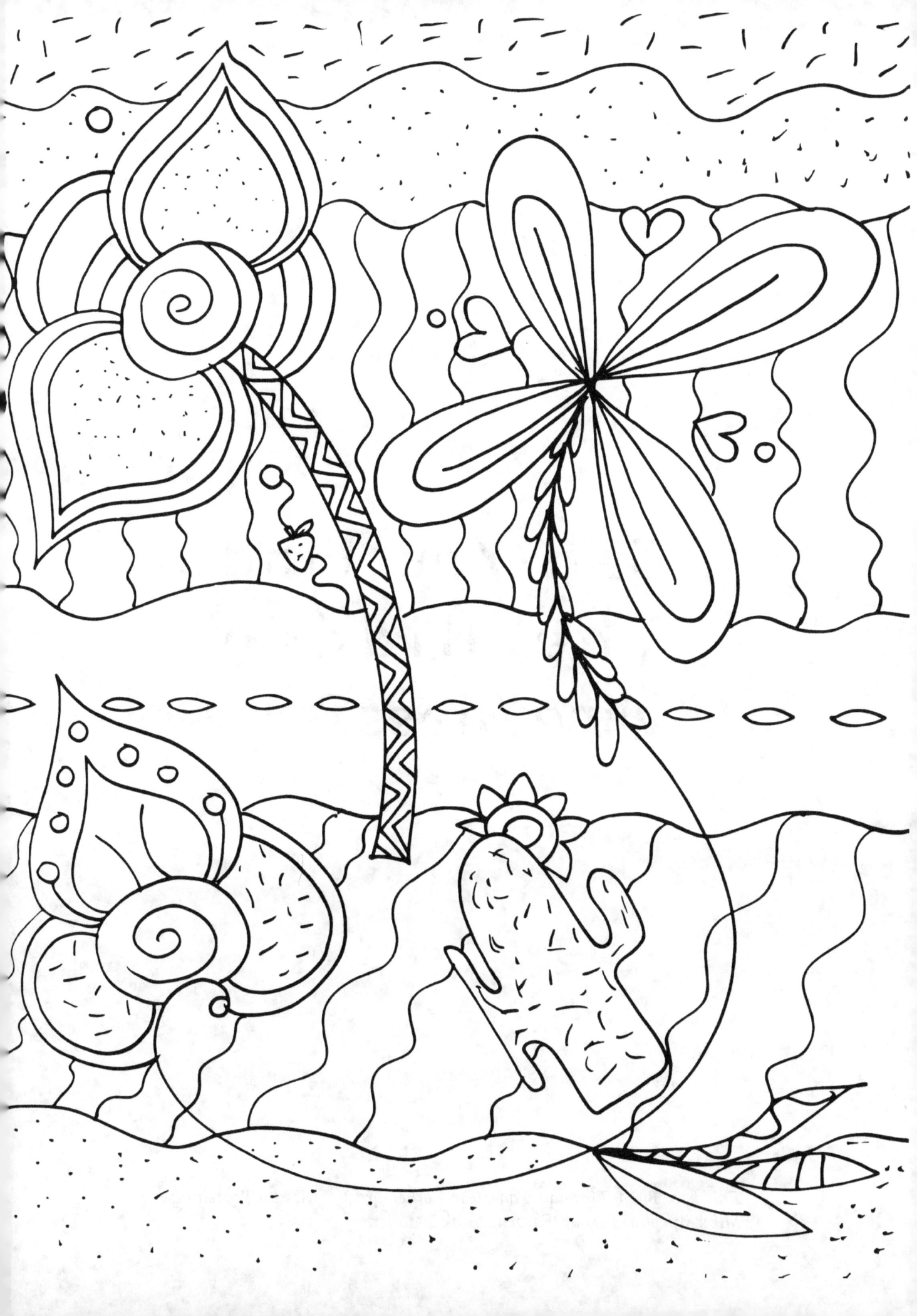

Can You Find The Hidden Wine Glass?

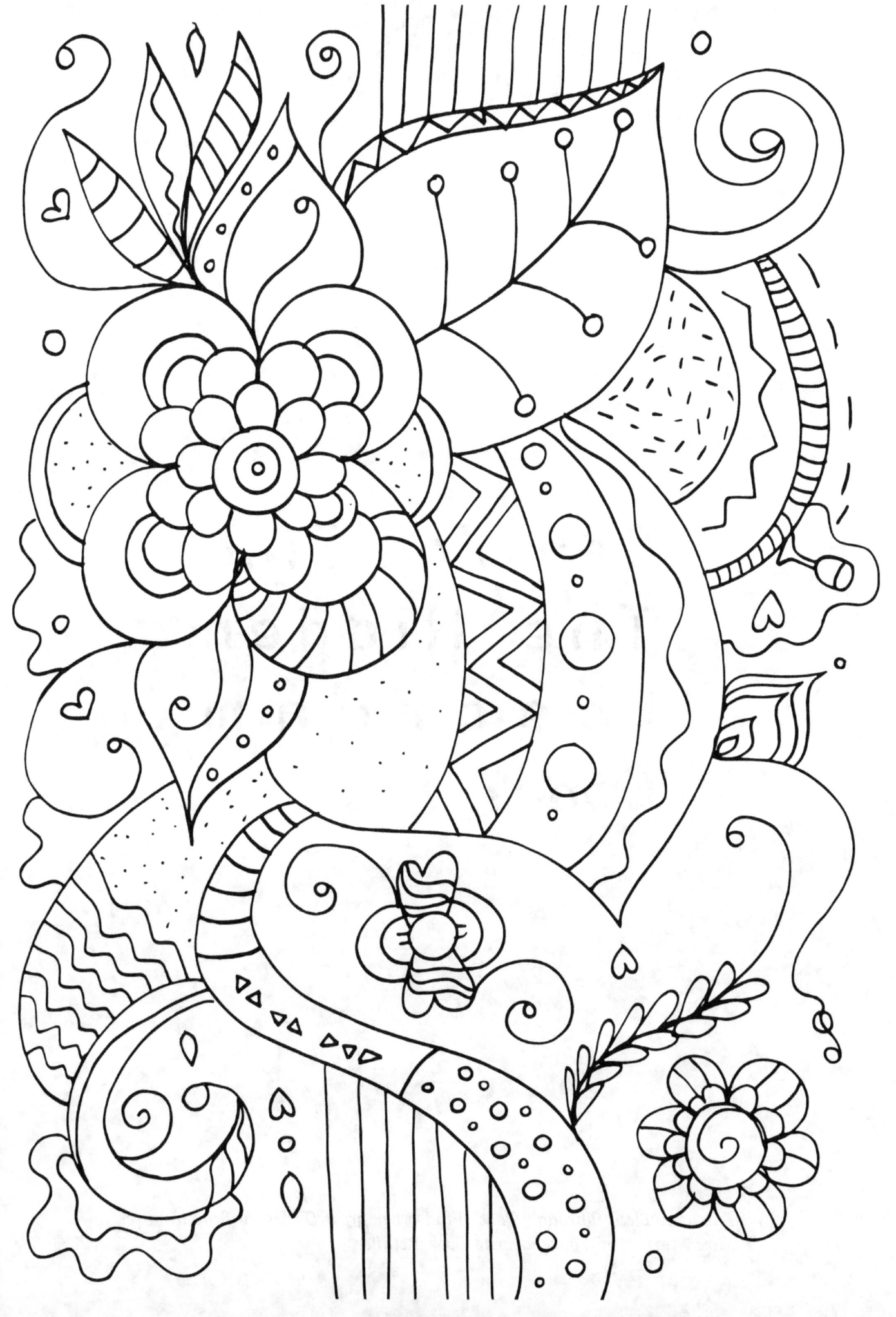

Can You Find The Hidden Icecream Cone?

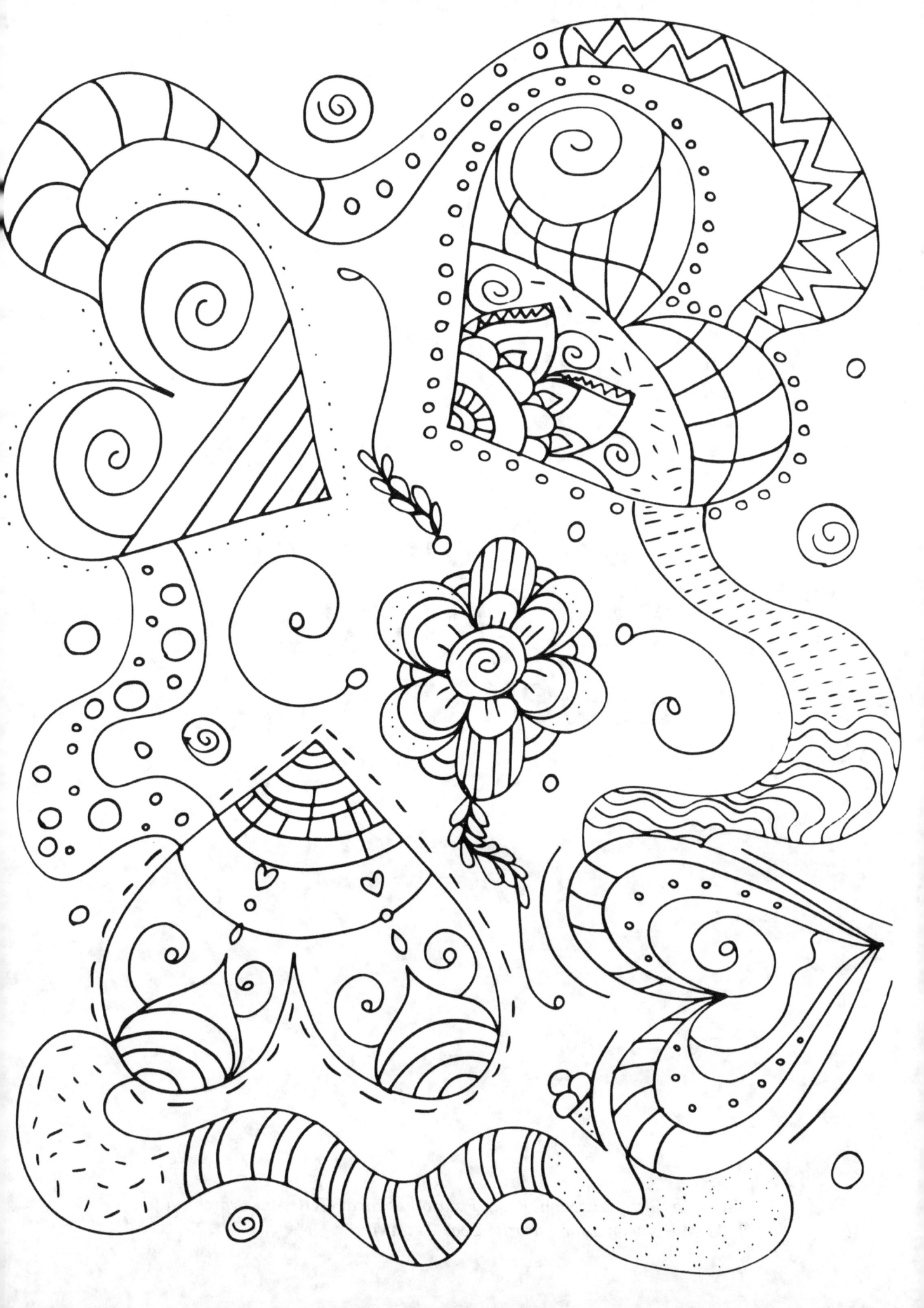

Can You Find The Hidden Bow?

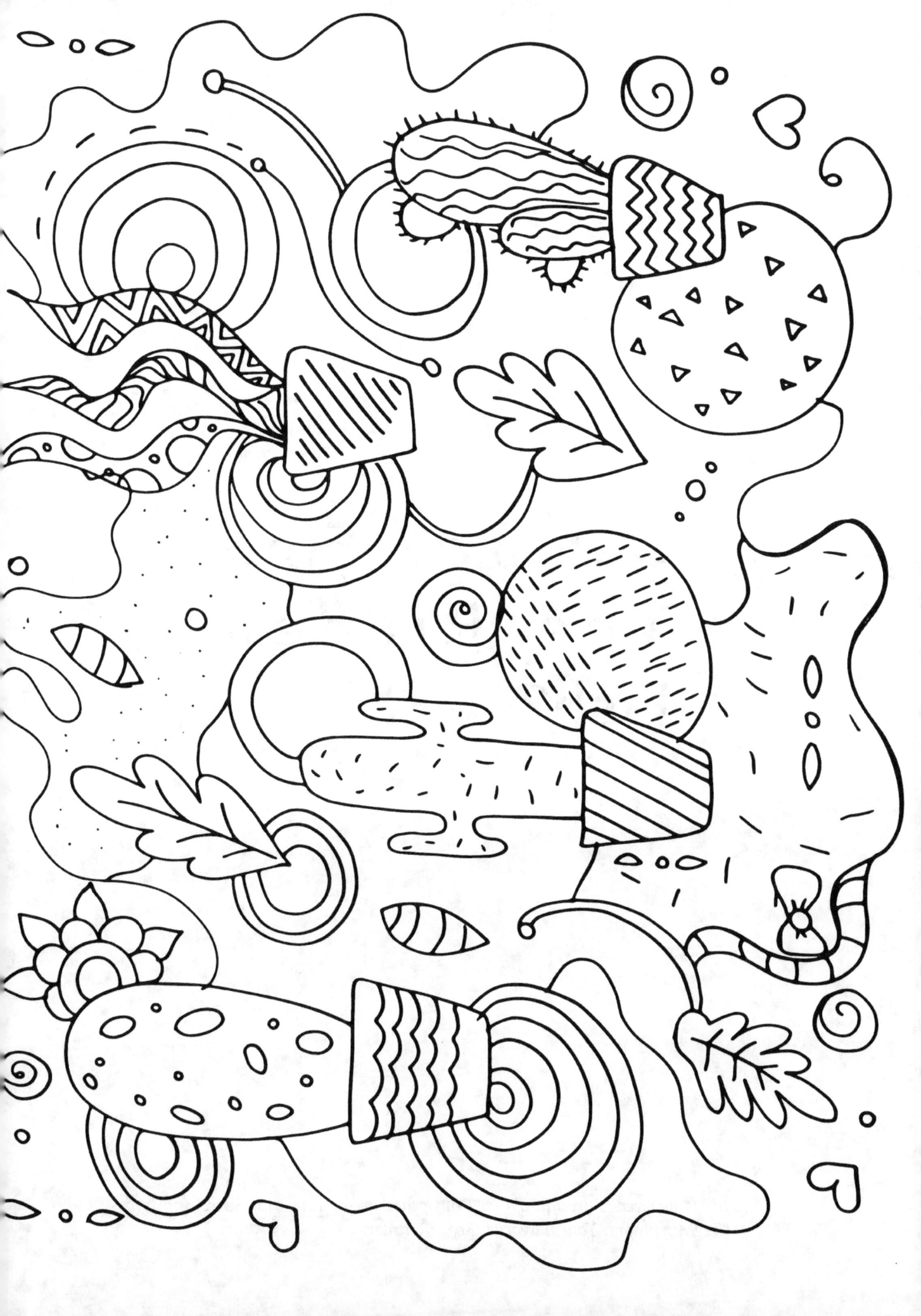

Can You Find The Hidden Fish?

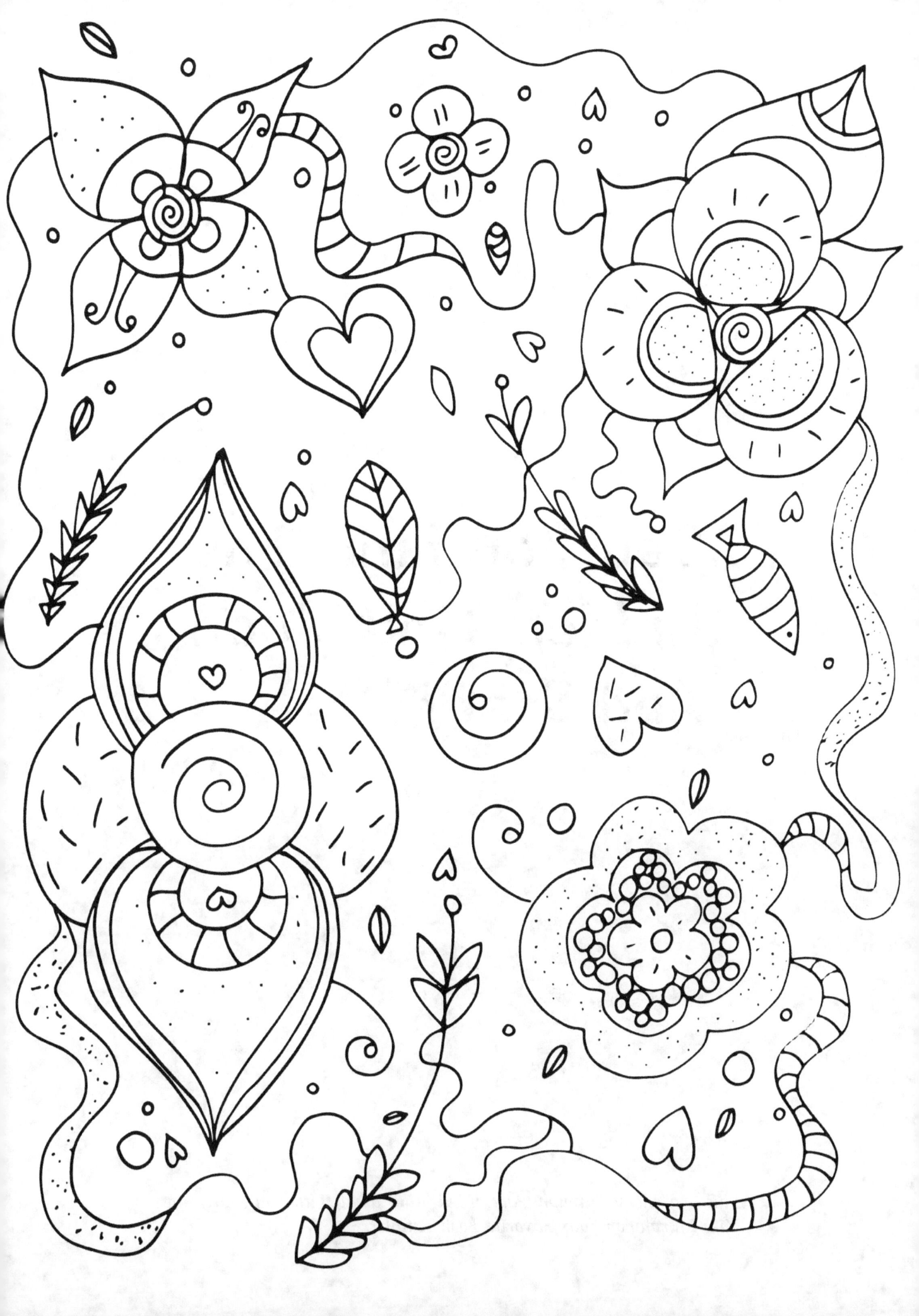

Can You Find The Hidden Tiny Moon And Star?

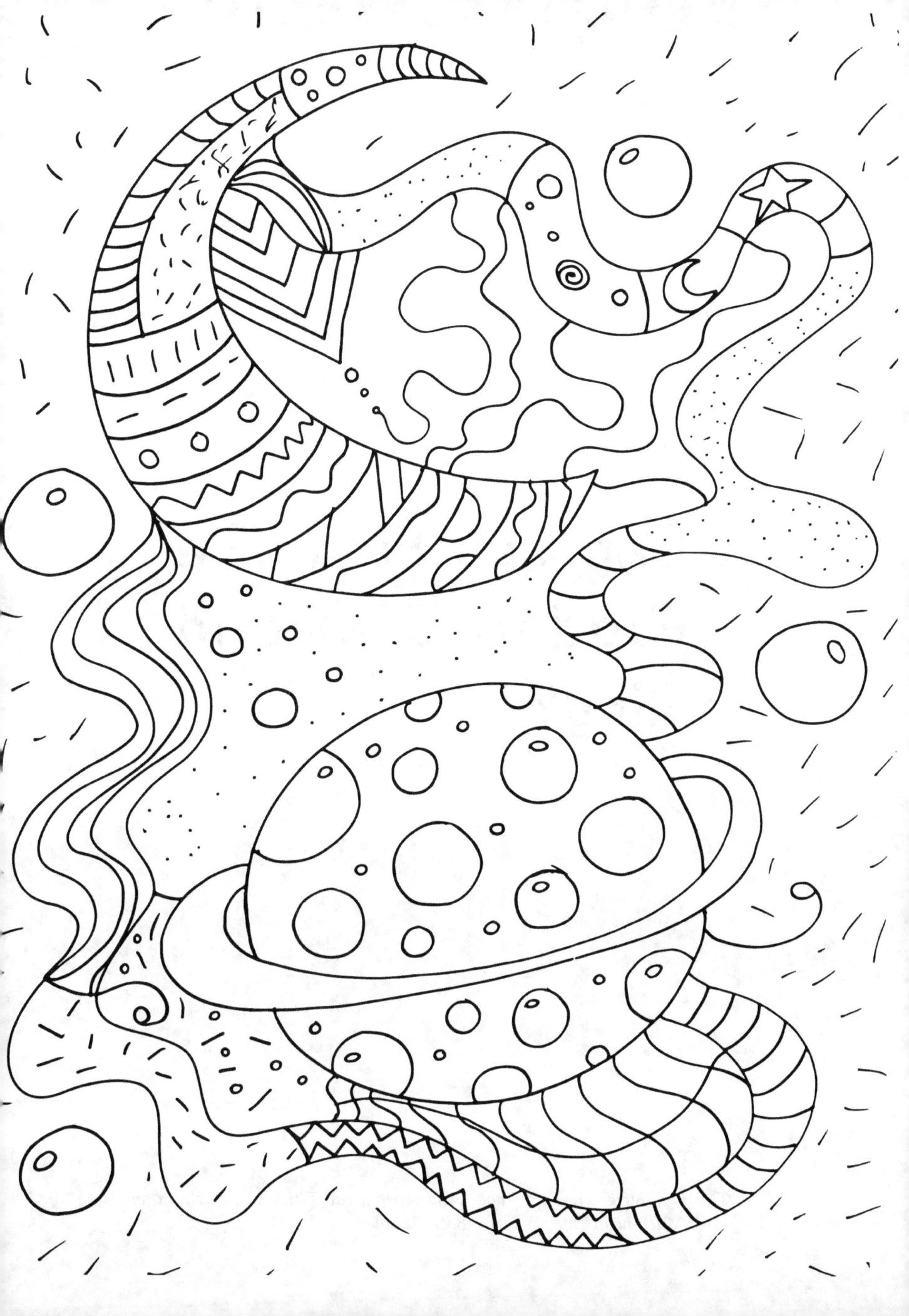

Can You Find The Hidden Diamond Ring?

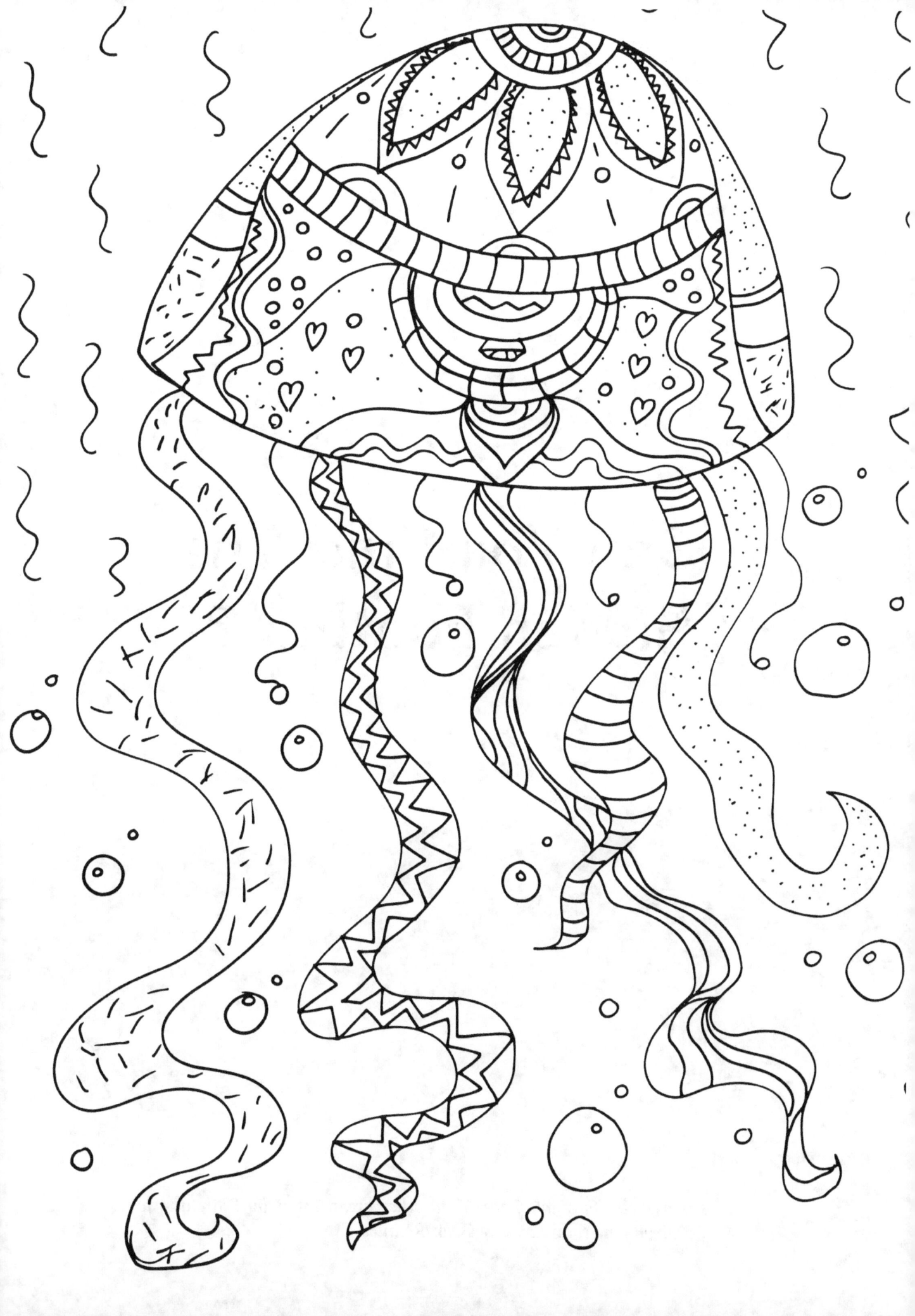

Can You Find The Hidden Football?

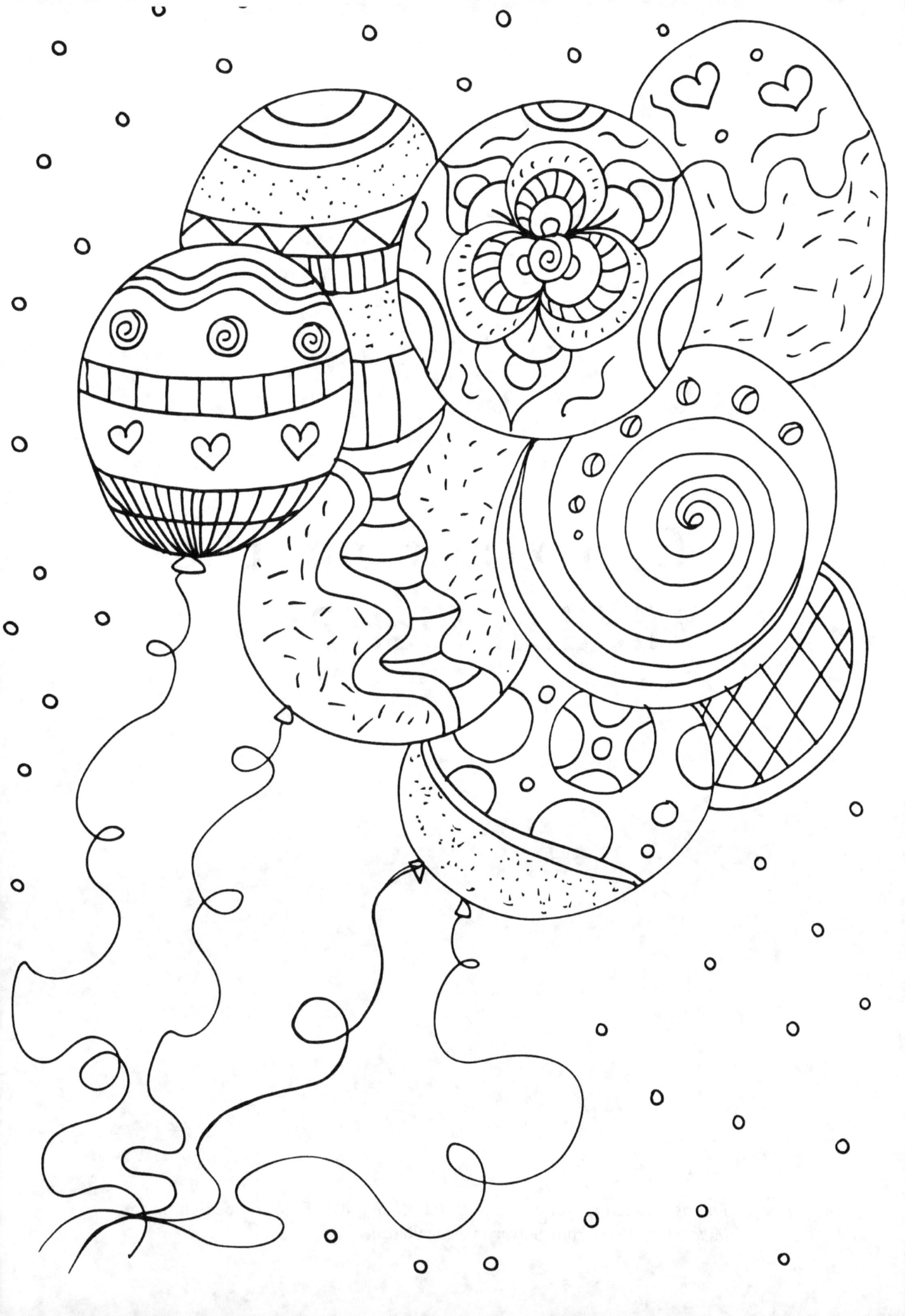

Can You Find The Hidden Fish?

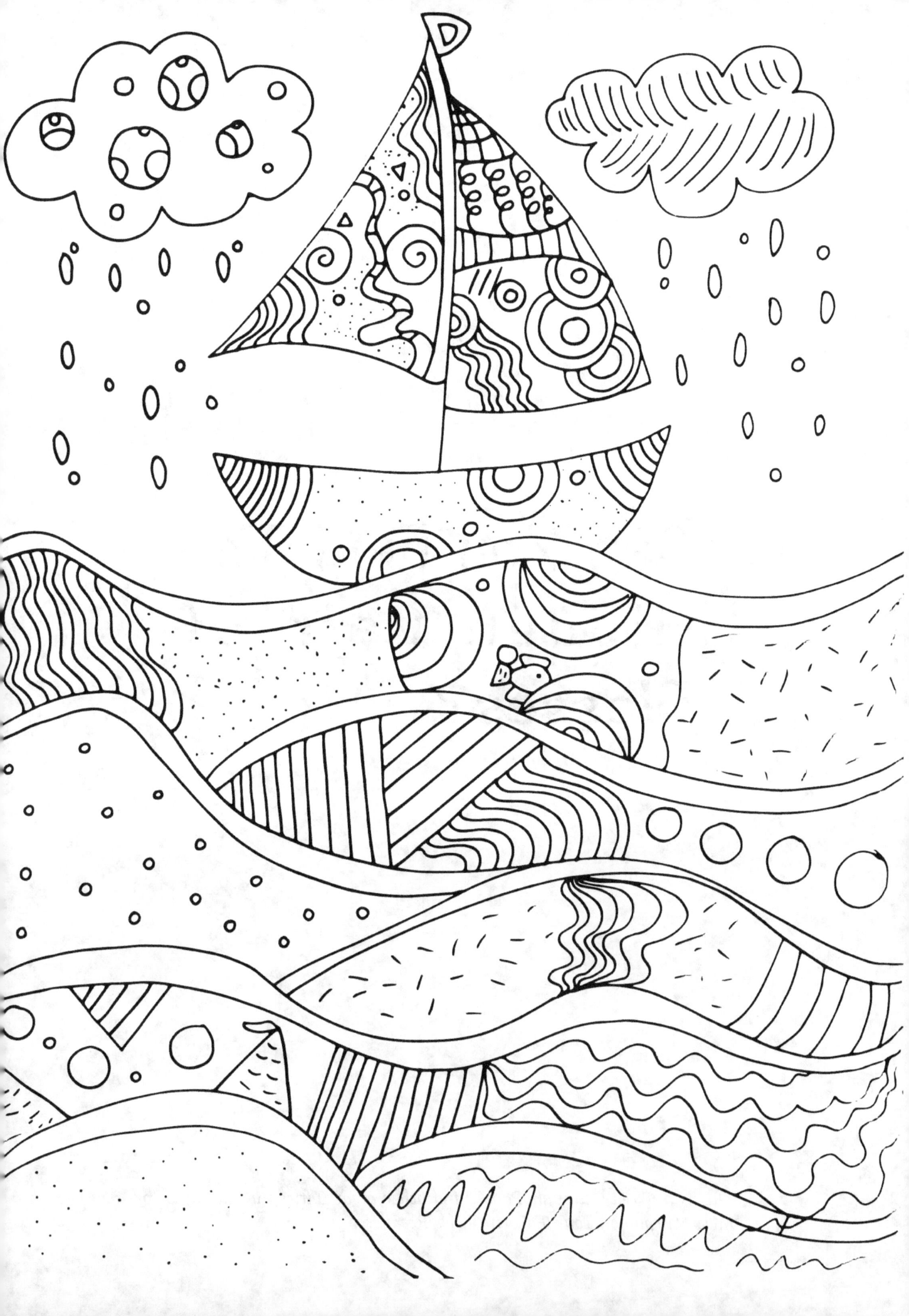

Can You Find The Hidden pair of Glasses?

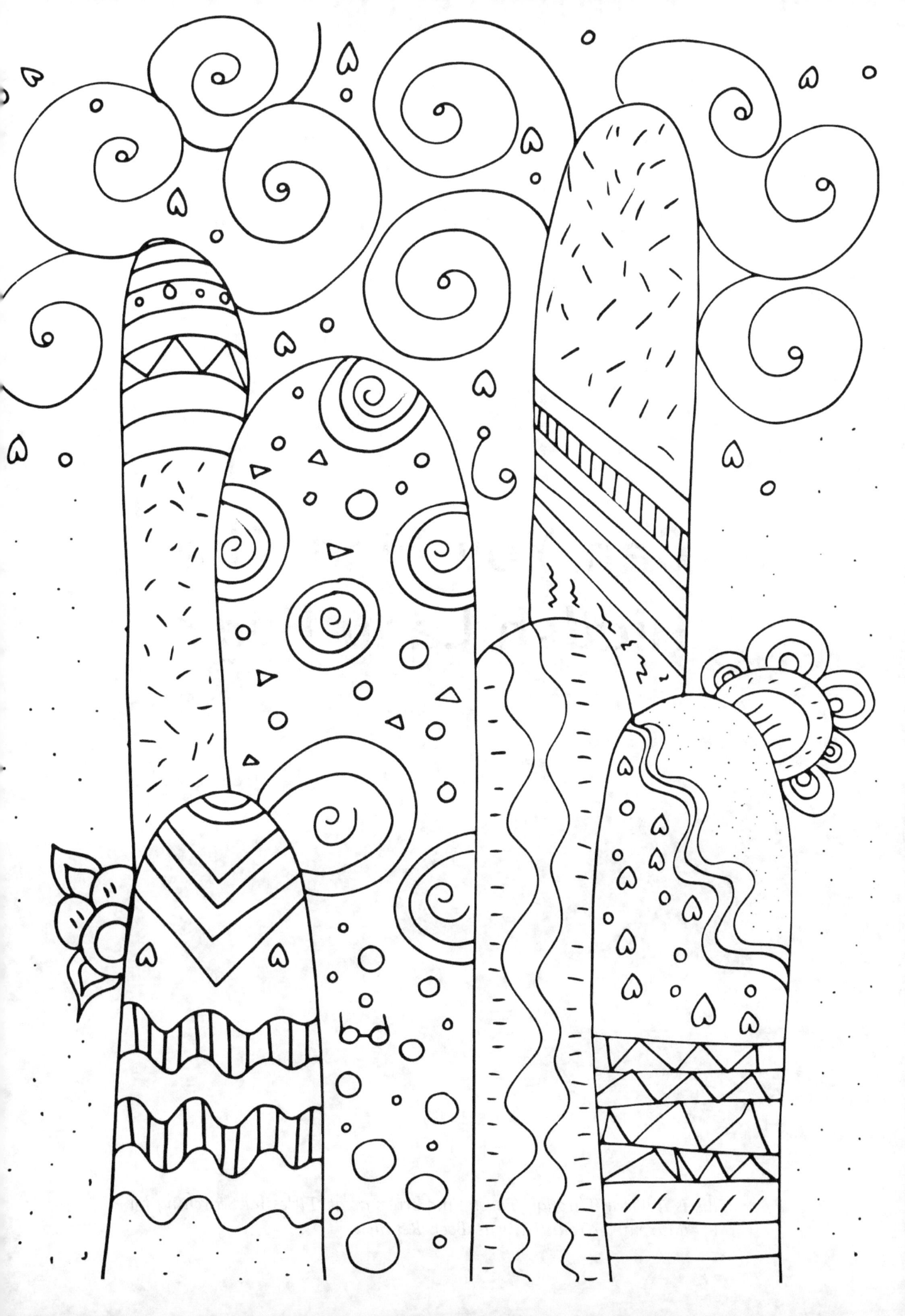

Can You Find The Hidden Lady Bug?

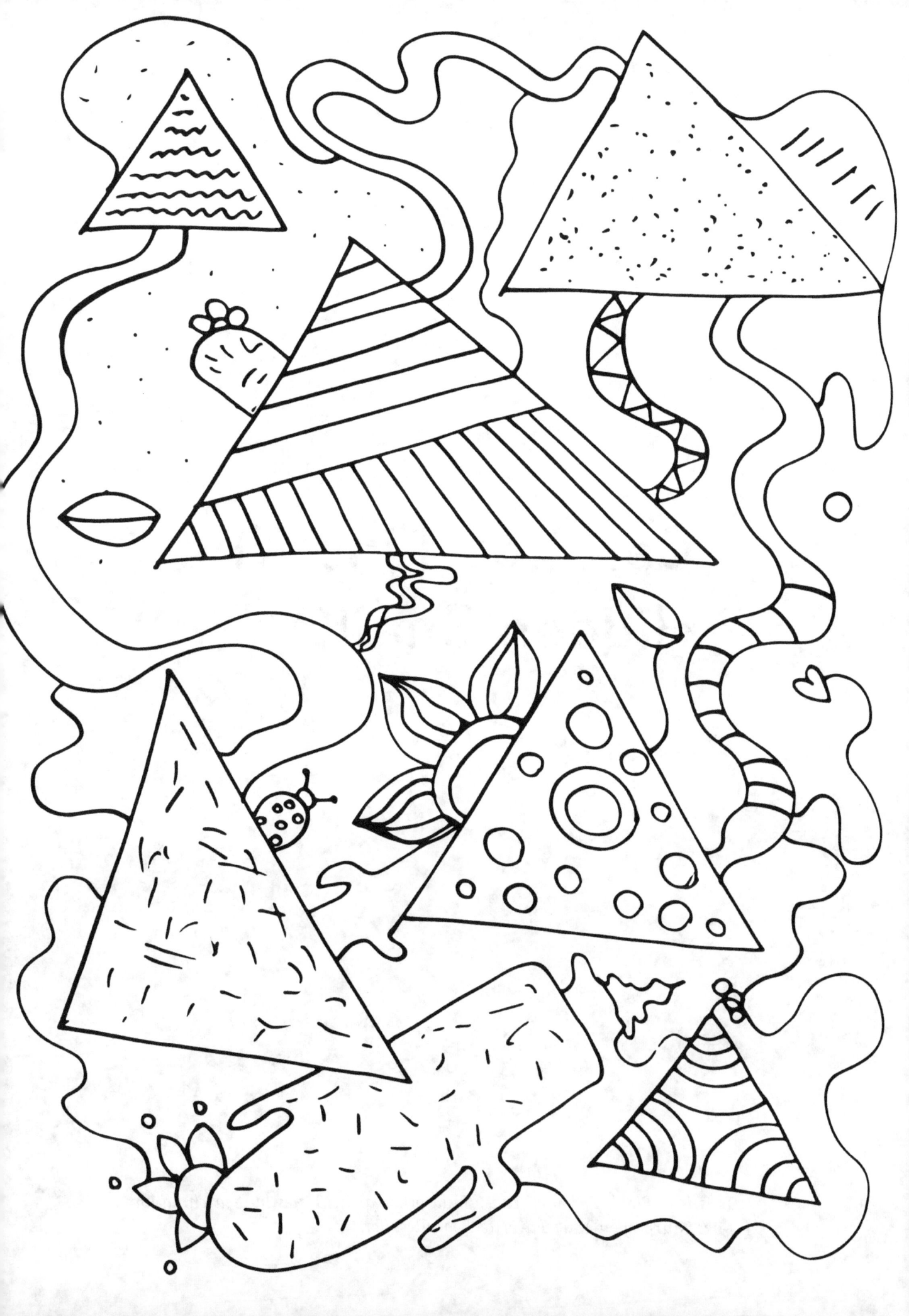

Can You Find The Hidden Snail?

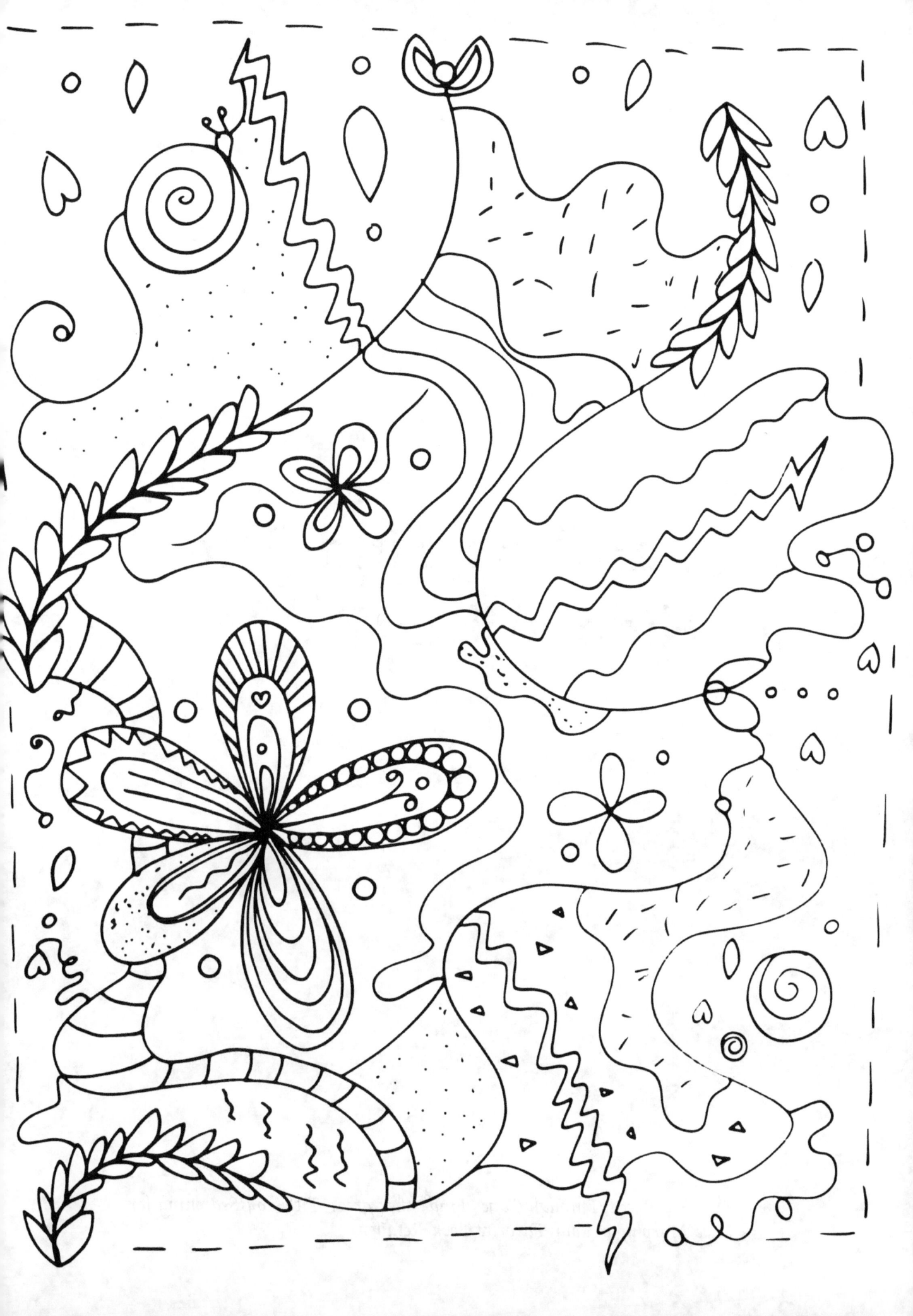

Can You Find The Hidden Key?

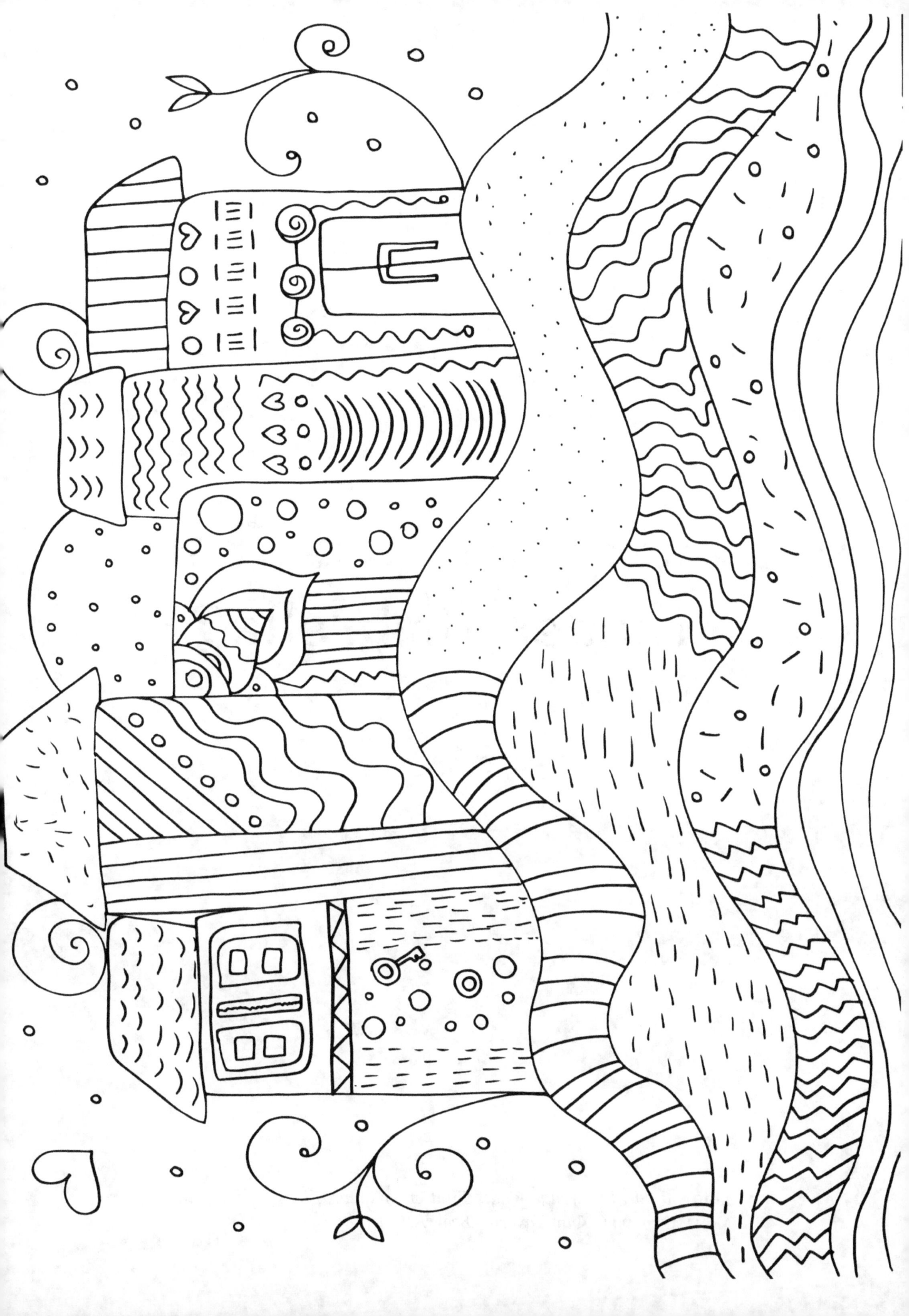

Can You Find The Hidden Umbrella?

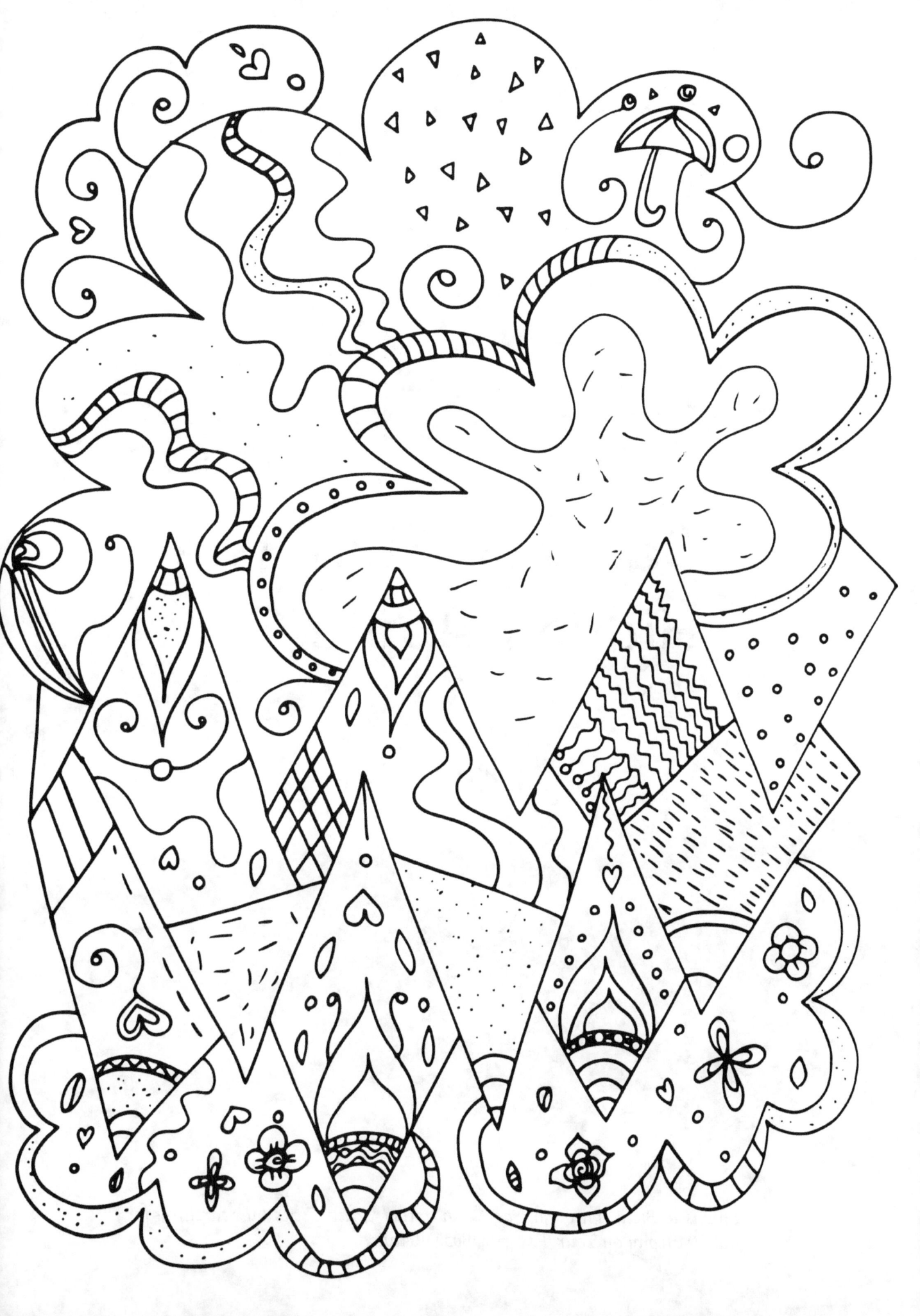

Can You Find The Hidden Apple ?

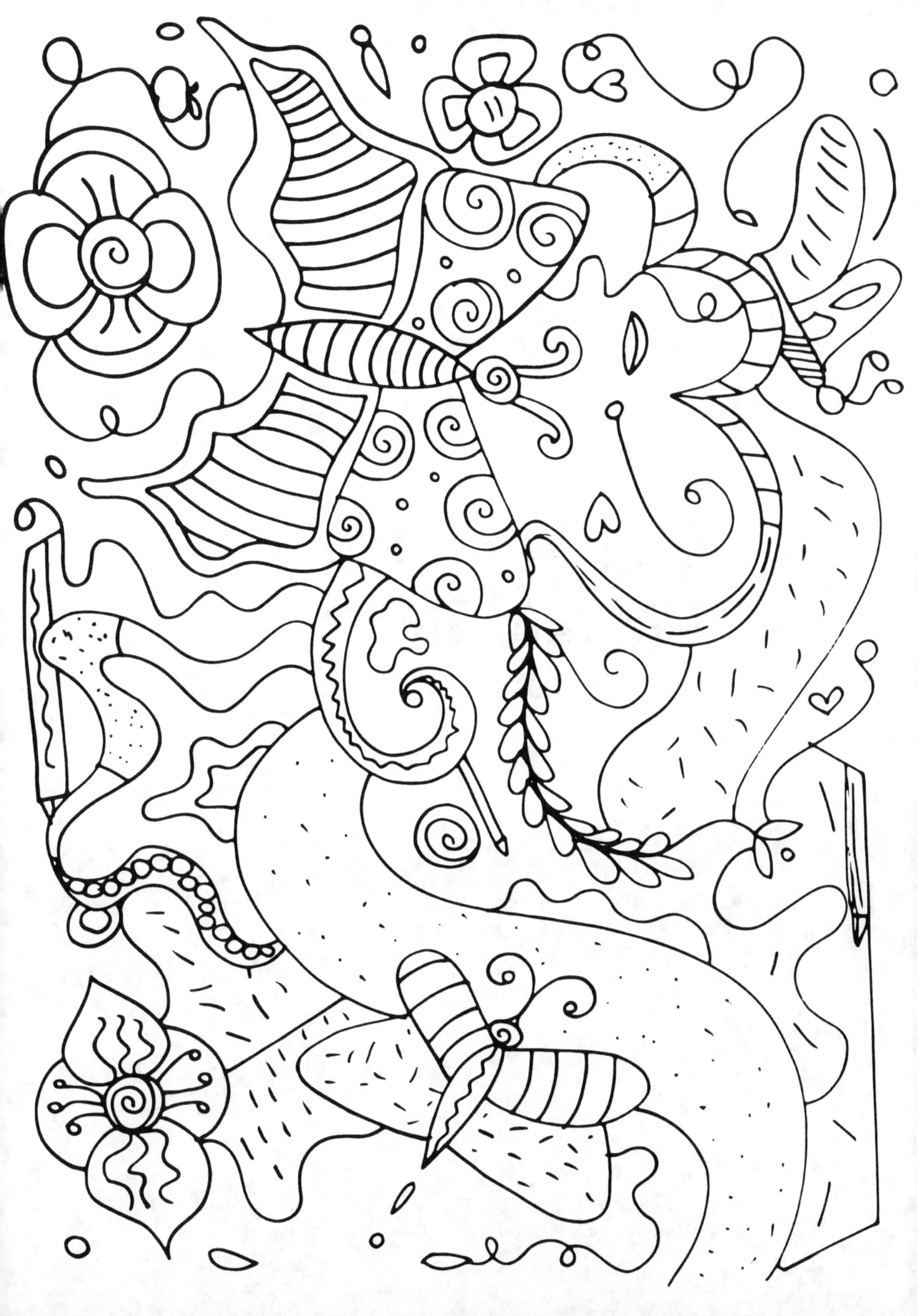

Can You Find The Hidden Bird?

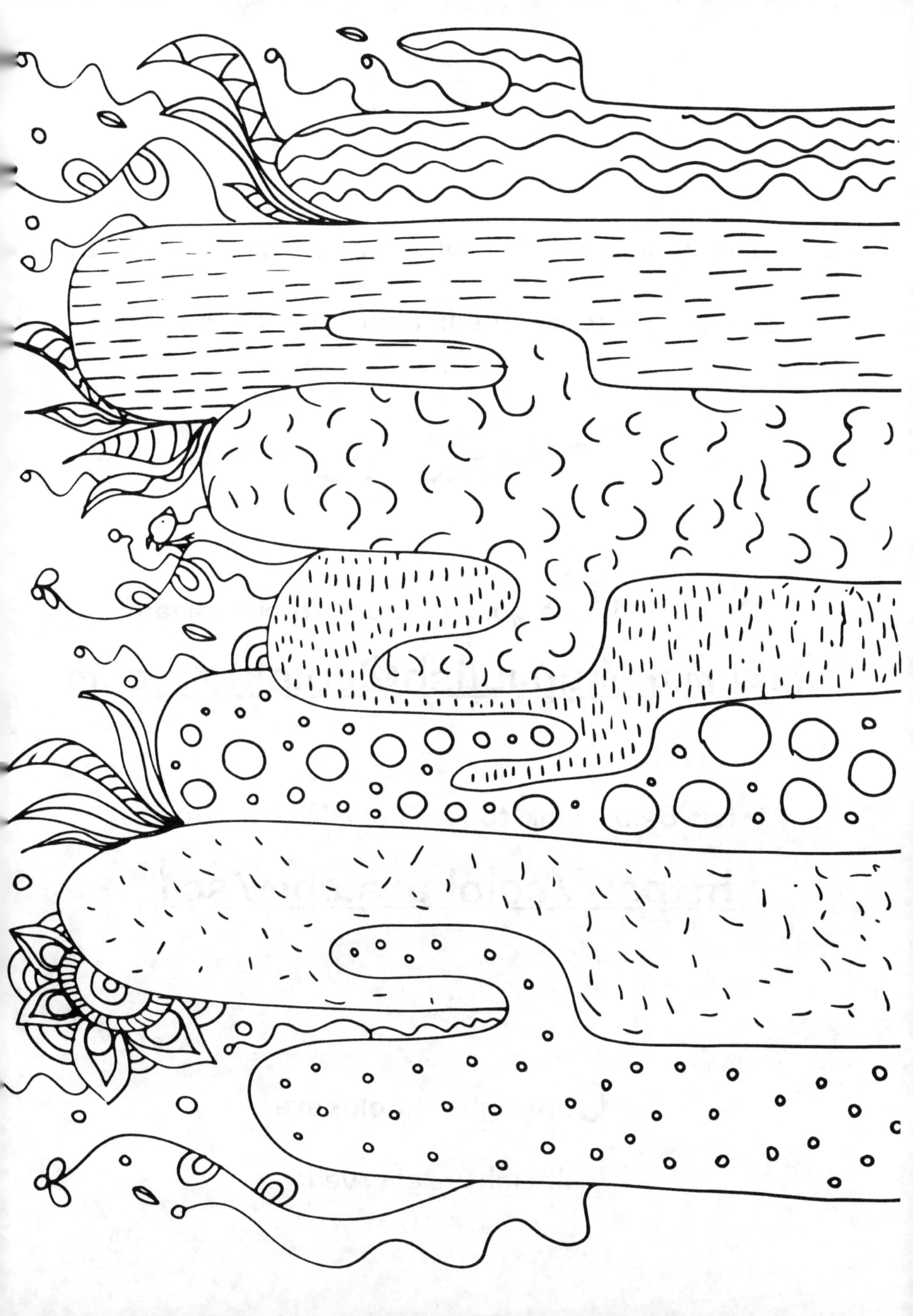

Please help to leave your review about this book so that u

can improve to make our next book even better.

Thank you!

Share with us your artwork to our e-mail:

mikemurphypublish@colokara.com

Visit Below Link to Get Your Digital Version

https://colokara.com/sc1